PHILOSOPHY OF RELIGION SERIES

Editor's Note

The philosophy of religion is one of several very active branches of philosophy today, and the present series is designed both to consolidate the gains of the past and to direct attention upon the problems of the future. Between them these volumes will cover every aspect of the subject, introducing it to the reader in the state in which it is today, including its open ends and growing points. Thus the series is designed to to be used as a comprehensive textbook for students. But it is also offered as a contribution to present-day discussion; and each author will accordingly go beyond the scope of an introduction to formulate his own position in the light of contemporary debates.

JOHN HICK

Philosophy of Religion Series

General Editor: John Hick, H. G. Wood Professor of Theology,
University of Birmingham

Published
*John Hick (Birmingham University) Arguments
for the Existence of God*
*H. P. Owen (King's College, London)
Concepts of Deity*
*Kaį Nielsen (Calgary University)
Contemporary Critiques of Religion*
*Terence Penelhum (Calgary University)
Problems of Religious Knowledge*
Forthcoming titles
*M. J. Charlesworth (Melbourne University)
Philosophy of Religion: The Historic Approaches*
*Ninian Smart (Lancaster University) The Phenomenon
of Religion*
*William A. Christian (Yale University)
Oppositions of Religious Doctrines:
A Study in the Logic of Dialogue among Religions*
*Basil Mitchell (Oriel College, Oxford)
The Language of Religion*
*Nelson Pike (California University)
Religious Experience and Mysticism*
Donald Evans (Toronto University) Religion and Morality
Dennis Nineham (Keble College, Oxford) Faith and History
*H. D. Lewis (King's College London) The Self and
Immortality*

Problems of
Religious Knowledge

TERENCE PENELHUM

MACMILLAN

First published 1971 by
THE MACMILLAN PRESS LTD
London and Basingstoke
Associated companies in New York Toronto
Dublin Melbourne Johannesburg and Madras

SBN 333 10633 4

Printed in Great Britain by
ROBERT MACLEHOSE AND CO LTD
The University Press, Glasgow

To Edith

Contents

Acknowledgements

George Allen & Unwin Ltd and Humanities Press Inc., New York, for the extract from 'Philosophical Papers' by G. E. Moore; Bobbs-Merrill Company Inc. for the extract from 'Philosophical Theology' by J. F. Ross; Columbia University Press for the extract from 'The Idea of Revelation in Recent Thought' by John Baillie; the extract from 'Faith and Knowledge' by John Hick, first edition © 1957, second edition © by Cornell University, used by permission of Macmillan & Co. Ltd and Cornell University Press; S.C.M. Press Ltd and Schocken Books Inc. for the extract from 'Metaphysical Beliefs' by Alasdair MacIntyre; S.C.M. Press Ltd and the Westminster Press for extracts from 'Aquinas on Nature and Grace' (The Library of Christian Classics, vol. xi), translated and edited by A. M. Fairweather, published in the U.S.A. by the Westminster Press, 1954; Professor Nicholas Rescher for the passage from 'Pleasure and Falsity' from 'American Philosophical Quarterly', vol. 1, no. 2, 1964; Professor George I. Mavrodes for the paper 'True Statements and Discursive Proofs', read to the American Philosophical Association at St Louis, May 1961.

1 Faith, Scepticism and Philosophy

(a) Preliminaries

My purpose in this book is to discuss some of the problems raised by the knowledge-claims made in religious faith and the rejection of these claims by religious sceptics. This disagreement, familiar to all of us, is one which raises for the philosopher both general issues in the theory of knowledge, and special problems connected with the unique subject-matter of claims to *religious* knowledge. In order to make clear what questions I shall be asking and what other questions I shall not be asking, I must first place this inquiry in the wider context of the philosophy of religion.

Philosophers have traditionally undertaken two main tasks when examining the claims of the Christian religious tradition. The first task has been that of coming to as clear an understanding of these claims as possible. Only a limited degree of success can be expected in this undertaking, since the subject-matter of much of religious discourse is said by its users themselves to be only partially accessible to human understanding. The second task, which is usually in prospect while the first proceeds, is that of evaluating the claims that the tradition makes; of deciding, as far as a philosopher is able to do, whether they are true. Most of what the reader will find here belongs to the first, rather than to the second, of these undertakings. We might refer to it as the descriptive task of philosophy, and the other as the evaluative task.

The descriptive task is one which should be able to proceed, or so it seems, without the philosopher who is engaged in it committing himself, as he describes Christian claims, to any view, positive or negative, about their truth. He may already have views about this, but it seems obvious enough that they need not intrude upon what he says while he is striving to make clear what the tradition actually proclaims. He can adopt, for professional purposes, a stance of philosophical neutrality — which means that what he says, as a philosophical analyst, about the content of religious

1

claims is religiously neutral and implies nothing about the truth of them. This is one obvious difference between a good deal of philosophical examination of religious beliefs, and the theological examination of them: even though theologians also spend much of their time in clarifying the meaning of our religious tradition, the theologian is committed, at least in general outline, to its truth, whereas the philosopher in his professional capacity is not. It may seem too obvious to be worth stressing that the descriptive task of philosophy is independent in this way from the evaluative one. Indeed, how can one even begin the task of evaluation without having completed the descriptive task, at least to the best of one's ability? Surely it is the fact that he does this first that makes it more likely that the evaluation a professional philosopher offers is worth the layman's attention? However obvious this may seem, it has been challenged in two opposing ways by contemporary philosophers of religion.

Both challenges begin from the same assumption: that different areas of human discourse have to be examined as they are, and should not be expected by philosophers to conform to standards that are found appropriate in others. Every sort of discourse, as the slogan goes, has its own sort of logic. Philosophers are felt to have expected one sort of discourse (such as moral discourse) to conform to standards that are appropriate only in some other (such as scientific discourse), and to have been bedevilled by perplexities of their own creation when such expectations have proved baseless and generated misunderstandings. The procedural Balkanisation of human thought and activity which results from trying to avoid this sort of error is due historically to the later work of Wittgenstein, and it has been enormously fruitful. But it is not always obvious what its implications are. When applied to religious discourse, it has led to two quite opposed results.

1. The first result has been the creation of a new form of religious scepticism, which we can call scepticism of meaning(1). Some philosophers have argued that, when examined, religious discourse is shown to be essentially incoherent. It uses ordinary expressions, they allege, but uses them in distorted and irrational ways. Believers, for example, say that God is intelligent or loving, but are not willing to

2

allow their claims about him to be tested by reference to what happens to those of his creatures towards whom God is said to exercise his care and providence. But this involves using language in two conflicting ways at once: in one way that arouses the normal expectations consequent upon the use of familiar terms, and in another way that explicitly frustrates them. But this can only show that religious discourse, when examined as it is, must be found to be dependent upon the perpetuation of mutually opposed modes of expression, and therefore not to be capable of being made intelligible when subjected to philosophical examination. If this contention is correct, then the descriptive task cannot be followed by the evaluative one, since one cannot first find out what religious claims mean and then decide on their truth. If they cannot be shown susceptible of clarification at all, then they lack a definite enough meaning for us to say that they are either true or false.

The discussion of the many complications raised by this form of attack on religious belief has been one of the major preoccupations of philosophy of religion within the last two decades, and it is the subject of other volumes in the series to which this one belongs. Such contributions to it as I have made are found elsewhere(2). Here I have to assume, without taking space to argue for it, that religious discourse can be shown to be sufficiently intelligible for us properly to go on to wonder whether it is true or not, and that there is a roughly coherent body of doctrine which the believer accepts and the sceptic denies. There will be echoes of the disputes about scepticism of meaning in what follows, but they will not be the centre of attention.

2. Scepticism of meaning has been matched on the other side of late by what has been called Wittgensteinian fideism(3). This also begins by assuming that each form of discourse has to be understood by itself, on its own terms. But it then proceeds to infer from this not only that a suitably comprehending examination of religious discourse will not result in scepticism of meaning, but also, much more radically, that a suitably comprehending examination prevents anyone from first deciding what religious claims are and then wondering whether they are true. Understanding

3

and participation are, the argument goes, necessarily connected, so that someone who wonders whether God exists or not does not understand what faith in God comes to. This position has paradoxical affinities with the Ontological Proof of God's existence, and also with some quasi-relativist views about the ability of anthropologists to understand primitive societies(4). It is tactically impregnable, since those who adopt this position can always insist that criticism must be based on misunderstanding. Criticism of religion often is based on misunderstanding, but it is the merest conversation-stopper to insist that it must necessarily be. While I shall refer to specific misunderstandings at intervals throughout this work, it will be part of my argument that believers and sceptics do not only have a common view of what the one accepts and the other rejects, but can, within limits, agree on what might resolve their disagreement, while continuing to disagree. I can only refer to the argument as it develops for grounds to support the view that understanding without participation is a possibility, and that not all debate about religion is at cross-purposes.

This brings us to the basic fact which makes Wittgensteinian fideism an irrelevant defence of religion. Whatever force it may have against forms of scepticism that result from philosophical misunderstandings of what religion is, the fact remains that scepticism about religion (unlike other forms of scepticism such as scepticism of the senses) is not something that philosophers have invented. It is something, like religion itself, that they find. It needs a great weight of argument to force us to hold, *a priori,* that what men of faith proclaim and what unbelievers deny is not one and the same thing, and known to be.

The task of this book can now be spelled out. It is that of making clear the nature of the disagreement between men of faith and sceptics. It is a descriptive task, but I shall attempt a description of both sides. I shall try to understand how each side looks to the other, and why, but shall try to avoid commitment to either side while I do this. The philosophical analyst must proceed by describing what he finds; but what he finds is a body of human discourse confronted by widespread rejection, not a body of discourse universally accepted. Within the Christian Church there is much concern about what it is that holds back so many from the Christian tradition at the present day, and how the Church should act in the face of such widespread rejection. Outside the Church there is of course no equivalent concern, but there is a parallel phenomenon: a widespread bewilderment that many men of intelligence and education should still retain allegiance to what seems to sceptics to be such an antiquated tradition. We can call this a barrier of incomprehension if we wish, and this is a natural way to speak of it. But in my view it is misleading to do this if it tempts us to think that the barrier is an indication of the influence of scepticism of meaning upon the religious situation. Scepticism of meaning is a serious intellectual challenge to Christianity, but it is parochial of philosophical sceptics, and of philosophically-oriented apologists, to imagine that it has played more than a peripheral role in the spread of religious scepticism. The fact that someone cannot understand how his neighbour can believe something does not show that he cannot understand that which his neighbour believes. It merely shows that it is strange to him that his neighbour should believe it. It is this actual division, and what lies on each side of it, that I want to examine. In doing so I shall assume that on the believer's side we have a believer who is concerned to maintain Christain doctrines in forms that permit him to accept all scientific advances but do not reduce to meaningless phrases when the appropriate disclaimers are made. No philosopher feels at ease about proceeding on big assumptions without arguing for them, but there is no alternative here.

I have said that I shall try to carry out the task I have outlined in a spirit of philosophical neutrality, and refrain from making evaluative commitments to one camp or the other. I shall have occasion to refer to the evaluation which each side makes of the other, and the arguments that each side has at its disposal, but one can indicate these things without espousing either side. As our title indicates, I shall not try to cover all the disagreements that divide believers from sceptics, for believers proclaim many things about moral matters, or matters of church government, and the like, and it is not these that will concern us. We shall be considering only claims that Christians make to knowledge of alleged facts about God and men's relationships to him, to the ways in which such claims are supported, and the reasons that are offered for their rejection by sceptics. This is of course artificial, as theologians frequently and properly remind us. The allegedly cognitive elements of religious faith interact in critically important ways with other features of it. Hence my account will include an attempt to outline the ways in which these elements in faith mingle with one another.

Since I have proclaimed philosophical neutrality, I must acknowledge three ways in which it has not been possible to proceed without compromising it in the eyes of some readers.

(i) I have put aside scepticism of meaning and Wittgensteinian fideism. I must now put aside something else. In evaluating religious beliefs, some philosophers have felt that these beliefs contradict one another. They have said, for example, that it is contradictory of believers to say both that God is all-good and all-powerful, and that evil exists in the world. This is not the same as scepticism of meaning: the argument now before us is not that religious language is incoherent so that there are no clear religious doctrines to believe, but that the doctrines are intelligible but in conflict with one another. If this criticism were true, no amount of evidence could possibly support, or refute, them as a whole. They would be ultimately self-refuting. This is one of the oldest criticisms of Christianity, but one which I cannot comment on here. I shall have to proceed as though Christian doctrines can not only be presented in forms that are compatible with modern scientific knowledge, but also in forms that are free of internal contradictions. While such generalisations are hazardous, I incline to the view that most sceptics do not deny that Christians can accommodate the facts of evil, for example, without falling into contradictions; they merely feel that the doctrinal devices they use to do so involve claims that there is no good reason to believe.

(ii) In evaluating religious beliefs, some philosophers have felt able to support them by offering proofs of the truth of some of them. Hence the famous traditional proofs of the existence of God. These are the subject of another volume in the present series, and I shall have to assume something controversial about them in order to proceed. To assume that

6

God's existence can be proved is to assume that God exists. To assume it cannot be proved is not to assume that God does not exist, but it is to assume some limitations on the way in which belief in God can be supported. I have argued elsewhere that the traditional proofs are all failures(5), and I shall take that as given. Many philosophers and theologians alike have assumed because of these failures that God's existence cannot be proved, though this is certainly a *non sequitur* as it stands. Catholic thinkers are committed to holding that God's existence can be known through natural reason, but this does not entail the soundness of any particular argument, and I would suggest that what follows is not necessarily impossible for a Catholic thinker to consider. I shall, in Chapter 2, examine the notion of a proof in a wholly general way, and in Chapter 3 look at the view that religious beliefs are incapable of proof. Although I accept this view, I do it with qualifications and hesitations, which remain in the background as the argument proceeds. While I do not think that adopting it prejudices the religious neutrality of my argument, especially in view of other things that I shall say, I must acknowledge that some may feel otherwise, and may even feel the same about the unargued assumption that no proofs of God's existence are forthcoming at the present time.

3. Finally, some theologians hold that it is impossible to have faith in anything but the truth, and that the suggestion that someone might have faith in what is false is a contradiction. If this should be true, then a philosophically neutral account of what faith is would be almost impossible to achieve; for if we assumed that there are any actual examples of faith, we would have assumed that whatever is held to by those who exemplify it is true, and therefore that God exists. I attempt to deal with this difficulty in Chapter 6, where I argue that we can proceed as though the faith we are examining has actual instances, without having to assume that what men of faith proclaim is true, and without having to reject those theologies that have a more restrictive concept of faith.

Our investigation will proceed as follows, In Chapter 2 I examine the nature of proof in general terms, and then proceed in Chapter 3 to the popular philosophical thesis that God's existence cannot be proved. I give this thesis a name

7

and adopt it, with reservations. This allows for a preliminary account of the gulf that divides believers from sceptics. In Chapter 4 I attempt a similar analysis of the nature of verification, which I use to assess the thesis of John Hick that Christian beliefs are verifiable. This permits an amplification of the earlier account of the disagreement between faith and scepticism. If religious belief is not to be founded on proof, it will depend upon revelation; Chapter 5 is devoted to an analysis of some aspects of this concept, which I do not assume to have instances. In Chapter 6 I conclude with a partial analysis of what faith is, with particular attention to the interrelationship between its cognitive and non-cognitive elements.

The argument is intended as an introduction to some of the central topics in what could be called the epistemology of religion. Even here there are major omissions: the intricate topic of religious experience is discussed only incidentally during the treatment of the concept of revelation, in part because the claims of religious experience are the subject of another projected volume in this series. I hope that the argument will at least provide a framework within which there can be further discussion of the many related issues that religious knowledge-claims raise. Since these cannot be understood without attention to many of the most general problems of epistemology, no apology is needed for the lengthy treatments of proof and verification in Chapters 2 and 4. The reader may, however, wonder at the outset why this work is confined as much as it is to description, and does not proceed to the second traditional task of evaluating religious claims. This question is answered by implication as the description proceeds. For the present, an allegory. Archimedes said that if he had a lever and a place to stand he could move the world. He could no doubt have gone on to say what length of lever and what place would be suitable. But he had no reason to think he could ever hold the lever, or go there.

(b) Two Accounts of Faith

In the remainder of this chapter I shall outline and contrast two accounts of the nature of religious faith and its relation to knowledge. The first is the traditional Catholic account that derives from St Thomas. On this view faith is a reasonable and free acceptance of certain propositions about God and man, belief in which is a prerequisite for salvation. The second is a modern Protestant account, deriving from the sixteenth-century Reformers and twentieth-century neo-orthodoxy, and placed in a philosophically accessible setting by Professor John Hick. On this view faith is a complex cognitive-conative response to God's alleged revelation of himself in human history. Each is a moderately complex view, embodying several distinguishable theses; consequently many other views of what faith is are possible, and have been held. Each, however, has the advantage of representing a major tradition in Christian theological thought, and of representing it in a form deliberately designed to facilitate philosophical analysis. The Reformed Protestant tradition has not often considered itself under an obligation to relate its major theological contentions to parallel philosophical debates, whereas St Thomas is conspicuous both for his desire to do this and his success in doing it. As a result, it seems best to choose a contemporary representative of the Protestant tradition, one of whose many valuable services to religious thought has been his capacity to do the same thing for it. This will avoid the hazards of inferring epistemological implications from non-philosophical writings. In one case, therefore, we shall be describing a position which is a primary source of a tradition, whereas in the other we shall be describing the position of one of its present representatives. The major expository gain from this procedure comes from the fact that each of our sources is a model of clarity and orderly presentation.

Let us begin, then, with St Thomas. The key to understanding his position on the nature of faith, as on so many other matters, is his assertion that grace does not supplant nature, but perfects it(6). Faith is one of the fruits of divine grace, but is at the same time a natural extension of activities of the human intellect that do not in themselves require it. For faith is essentially a matter of assenting to certain propositions which, though they cannot be arrived at by reason alone, it is nevertheless reasonable to assent to

9

because certain others can be known to be true by reason alone. The two groups of propositions form the subject-matter, respectively, of revealed theology and natural theology. In natural theology, which is, in spite of its title, part of philosophy, one begins with premises which are accessible to natural reason, and reaches conclusions about God and his relation to the world. These conclusions, though they must be held to for a man's salvation, are nevertheless demonstrable by reason without the aid of revelation. In revealed theology, however, reason is confined to systematising and drawing conclusions from premises which natural reason cannot discover. They have to be learned through revelation alone, and held on faith. The acceptance of them, however, is shown to be reasonable by the very fact that the propositions of natural theology can be demonstrated first. While faith is not tentative acceptance, but wholehearted acceptance, of revealed truths, it is not irrational, since someone who has learned the truths of natural theology (for example, that God exists and is one) can then reasonably give voluntary assent to the truths of revelation (for example, that God is a unity of three Persons, and was incarnate in Jesus Christ). Of course most men do not have the time or training or wit to follow the arguments of philosophers, and for them even the truths with which natural theology deals are learned from revelation: God would not leave men to discover truths of such importance through a discipline with such a limited audience. All men need to hold most Christian truths by faith, since those that reason can learn independently are not in themselves sufficient for salvation. In spite of this, however, the assent which the faithful freely give to the truths revealed to them is shown to be a rational assent because grounds for expecting God to have revealed them can be found in natural theology by those qualified to search.

I shall now attempt to list more formally the various theses that go to make up St Thomas's account of faith and its relation to knowledge.

1. Faith is a form of assent to propositions. Aquinas makes this very clear in his account of faith in the 'Summa Theologica', Secunda Secundae, Questions 1-7. In Article 2 of Question 1 he states that the human intellect knows truth by means of the 'combination and separation of ideas', so that even though, as the first sentence of the Apostle's Creed indicates, the object of faith is God himself, 'from the point of view of the believer the object of faith is something complex, in the form of a proposition'. So having faith in God is assenting to propositions about him.

2. *Revelation is of propositions.* 'For the faith of which we are speaking does not assent to anything except on the ground that it is revealed by God'. (S.T., IIa IIae, Q.1, Art. 1) Faith and revelation are correlative notions, in that what one assents to in faith is something one accepts because God has revealed it. What God has revealed is a body of truths, and he has revealed them in the Scriptures and in the doctrinal pronouncements of the Church. It seems to follow from this account of faith that one cannot have faith in false propositions. This is the burden of Article 3, where he argues that one cannot have faith in something false.

3. *The assent which characterises faith is not tentative, but wholehearted.* Although the propositions which one accepts in faith are not propositions which are demonstrated, and are therefore propositions which one can refuse to accept, they are not held to in the tentative way in which one might adopt some explanatory theory. Faith is placed by St Thomas midway between knowledge and opinion. He makes this distinction very clearly in the following passage:

> ... faith implies intellectual assent to that which is believed. But there are two ways in which the intellect gives its assent. In the first way, it is moved to give its assent by the object itself, which is either known in itself, as first principles are obviously known, since the intellect understands them, or known through something else that is known, as are conclusions which are known scientifically. In the second way, the intellect gives its assent not because it is convinced by the object itself, but by voluntarily preferring the one alternative to the other. If it chooses with hesitation, and with misgivings about the other alternative, there will be opinion. If it chooses with assurance, and without any such misgivings, there will be faith. (IIa IIae, Q.1, Art. 4)

I take the unhesitatingness to refer primarily to the manner in which the proposition is held, rather than to the length or manner of the process of decision leading to its acceptance. Faith then differs from knowledge in being determined in part by the choice of the believer, and from opinion in being held without misgiving. It is a free and wholehearted assent to the propositions believed.

4. *Though the assent is voluntary, it has a rational basis.* Although, as Hick emphasises, there seems some ambiguity in the Thomist position on this matter, there is no doubt that Aquinas considers the assent of faith to have strong grounds(7). The grounds are the truths which constitute the preambles to faith. These include on the one hand the demonstrations of God's existence, unity and the like, and on the other the historical evidences of the authority of the Church. The demonstrations give us knowledge (which would seem to imply that they compel assent), though the other preambles suffice merely to make it reasonable to assent to what the Church proclaims, without giving it demonstrative certainty. There is, then, a necessary connection between the voluntariness of faith (and its meritoriousness) and the fact that the propositions to which one gives assent in faith are not propositions which we can prove:

> The assent of one who knows scientifically does not depend on his free will, since the cogency of demonstration compels him to give it. Hence, in science, assent is not meritorious ... (S.T., IIa IIae, Q.2, Art. 9 ad 2)

> ... he who believes has a sufficient reason for believing. He is induced to believe by the authority of divine teaching confirmed by miracles, and what is more, by the inward prompting of divine invitation. Hence he does not believe lightly. But he does not have a reason such as would suffice for scientific knowledge. Thus the character of merit is not taken away. (ad 3)

5. *The rational basis lies partly in the fact that some truths about God can be demonstrated.* In these cases, of course, it is knowledge that one gets as a result of the demonstrations, as we have seen above.

6. *Faith and knowledge are exclusive.* Aquinas believes that the matters to which we assent in faith are mysteries, that is, are truths which we are not only incapable of learning

without their being revealed to us, but which we cannot in this life understand. The nature of God is in itself fully intelligible, but not to us, though we are promised that the dimness of our present understanding will be superseded hereafter by a clearer vision. Hence the intrinsic certainty of divine truths does not yield us knowledge in this life(8). But the mutual exclusiveness of faith and knowledge follows independently from the necessary connection thought to obtain between the freedom of assent in faith and the absence of conclusive demonstration for its articles. There is a residual problem regarding those propositions necessary for salvation that are contained within natural theology and are therefore capable of being known through natural reason. Clearly most men do not learn of them through reason, but hold them on faith. St Thomas deals with this by holding that one and the same proposition can be known by one man and held on faith by another man, but cannot be both known and held on faith by the same person(9). It follows from this that someone who begins holding God's existence, for example, on faith, and then comes to recognise the demonstration of it, replaces his previous faith in this proposition by knowledge of it.

The Thomistic view of faith, with its distinction between natural and revealed theology, has been normative for many generations of Catholic thinkers. (It was in fact given even greater authority than ever by the Vatican Decrees of 1870, where it is required that all believers hold, presumably in advance of the relevant philosophical demonstrations in most cases, that natural knowledge of God can be had through reason. 'If any one shall say that the one true God, our Creator and Lord, cannot be certainly known by the natural light of human reason through created things: let him be anathema'(10). It is only fair to point out that this only commits Catholics to the view that reason can lead us to knowledge of God, and does not commit them to the acceptance of any particular demonstration of his existence.) Thomas's account of faith has been the target of severe criticism both from philosophers and theologians. The philosophical criticism has centred, of course, upon the enterprise of natural theology. The individual arguments for God's existence and for propositions about God's nature and

13

relationship to the world that Thomists and other natural theologians have produced have been subjected to both general and specific attacks. The general attacks have been on the very enterprise of proving claims of this kind, which critics have said to be beyond the scope of the human intellect. The specific attacks have been on the details of the proofs themselves, which have generated many volumes of discussion and are likely always to continue to do so. The most important historical sources of both the general and the specific criticisms of natural theology are to be found in the writings of Hume and Kant. It does not lie within the scope of this volume to discuss the specific criticisms, though I shall shortly be commenting on the general ones. I can only say here what I have argued elsewhere, that the theistic proofs known to me seem to me to be failures.

It is easy to dismiss theological criticism of the enterprise of natural theology as an attempt on the part of Christian thinkers to make a theological virtue out of a philosophical necessity. This, however, would be quite unfair historically: theological scepticism about the value of the proofs has a long ancestry, and the main source of such criticism has been the Protestant tradition, which, quite apart from its tendency to distrust philosophy in any case, has independent reasons for being unreceptive to the enterprise of establishing religious truths by means of it. These include not only objections to the attempt to prove God's existence, but also a different understanding of the nature of the faith to which such an enterprise is thought by St Thomas to be a preliminary, and a different understanding of the nature of the revelation on which faith is held to depend. The Protestant tradition, especially as we find it in Kierkegaard and Karl Barth, emphasises that the gulf which human sin places between man and God is one that shows itself not only in human actions, but also in human thought-processes, so that man as a sinner is incapable of attaining to knowledge of God on his own account, without the intervention of divine grace. Attempts to use devices such as philosophical demonstrations to gain such knowledge are attempts to do by human means something that can only be done by God in his grace, and to represent as acceptable by human standards something which is a radical departure from them. For faith,

14

Protestants emphasise, is a radical decision, and involves a commitment which men have no right to hedge round by demonstrations that it is really reasonable. There has often been a tendency to flaunt what is said to be the absence of human grounds for the leap of faith, and to stress how far the pilgrimage of faith is from making good sense in human terms; but we need not explore this tendency here. It is enough to note that the enterprise of natural theology has been criticised in the Protestant neo-orthodox tradition as sinful in its motive, doomed to fail in its intent, and distorted in its view of what faith is. This alleged distortion is further said to derive from the fact that faith is not, as St Thomas argues, as matter of assent to propositions at all. It is rather a response of trust and commitment to God himself. The Protestant insistence that men's relation to God need not be mediated through the Church has here taken the form of questioning the interpretation of faith as an assent to the Church's pronouncements. Faith is trust in God. In twentieth-century versions at least, this has been thought to entail a different view not only of faith but also of revelation. Revelation is said not to be the proclamation of propositions about God, but to be the revelation of God himself. This has taken place through historical events and actions, in particular the history of Israel and the life of Christ. The Scriptures are therefore not infallible records of truths which God tells us about himself, but historical accounts of the revelatory events in history through which God has made himself known to men, and of men's responses to those events. Through them and through the continuing tradition which they began, men can themselves come to know of God and can come to decide to respond to him in trust.

The gulf between this understanding of what faith is and the interpretation of it that derives from St Thomas is in some ways very wide. One notable result of this difference is the relative absence of creedal declarations in the Protestant tradition: since doctrines represent interpretations of what God has revealed, and do not themselves consist of what God has revealed, it is not always assent to them which is critical in determining whether someone possesses the faith or not. On the other hand, certain facts of logic cannot be gainsaid. One of these is the fact that one cannot regard some historical event or personality as being revelatory without making some interpretation of it, even if there is latitude over which interpretation one makes. The other is that trust, like all interpersonal attitudes, entails some beliefs about its alleged object. It is logically impossible to say, with truth, that Smith is grateful to Jones without entailing that Smith at least believes that Jones has done him some service. It is not possible, in logic, to say that Smith is envious of Jones without entailing that Smith at least believes Jones to be, or to have, something which Jones is not, or does not have. Similarly it is not possible, in logic, to say that Smith trusts God without entailing that Smith believes that God cares for him, that God is steadfast, and the like - in short, one cannot be said to trust someone unless one is also said, or implied, to believe that the being towards whom one has this attitude has qualities or performs actions which make him worthy of being the object of it. Furthermore, of course, no one, in logic, can be said to trust a being whom he does not believe to exist. So the man of faith necessarily believes certain things about God, and necessarily interprets those elements in his experienced world which he regards as revelatory. So even if faith in God is not assent to propositions, it is a highly propositional activity. It is very foolish to exaggerate the differences between the two positions we have outlined to the point of suggesting that the second dispenses with the propositional elements of the former.

Nevertheless the necessity of interpretation and of commitment to propositions does not prove that the propositions to which faith commits one can be justified independently of the faith itself. To insist that this must be possible is to demand that traditional natural theology should deliver the sort of result which, on this view, there are theological reasons for thinking it cannot deliver. So while someone who claims to have encountered God's revealing activity may perhaps be able to justify other beliefs and decisions that he adopts by reference to this alleged encounter, there would be no way of offering independent justification of the whole complex of beliefs and decisions. The claim of natural theology to provide an independent justification is firmly rejected.

In John Hick's 'Faith and Knowledge' (11) we find an

account of faith which, while deriving from the Protestant tradition, makes the logically necessary concessions to the propositional nature of such a human attitude. Hick characterises faith as the 'interpretative element in religious experience'(12). He rejects the claims of natural theology to prove the existence of God, largely upon the ground that human freedom to choose whether or not to make the commitment of faith would be jeopardised if proof were possible. The alleged fact that suggests the enterprise of proof must fail (that God offers knowledge of himself that men are free to take or refuse) shows that divine revelation will have been vouchsafed to us - though in a form that does not compel human acceptance. Revelation is in the form of 'saving events', such as the history of Israel and the life of Christ. These events, however, can be given a wholly secular interpretation, as well as the interpretation that treats them as revelatory; for they are alleged to be events in history and are therefore subject to the ordinary canons of historical investigation and explanation. The theistic reading of them is, therefore, an optional one, in the sense that a man is free to accept or reject it, and his rejecting it cannot be dismissed, as the natural theologian would have us dismiss it, as irrational. This, however, does not show that the theistic interpretation of these events is not itself a rational one. It is of course extended beyond the specially revelatory events to include the whole of the life and experience of the believer. For the whole of life can, if we elect to do this, be seen as an ongoing encounter with God. To see it as this is to have faith. Faith interpreted in this way can be seen to include, but not to require, the more exceptional and dramatic forms of religious experience; for in essence faith is a way of seeing the whole of the subject's experience. Faith is optional, but not irrational, for if the propositions to which it commits one are true, there is every reason to expect our relationship to God to be optional in this way. Finally, faith is subject to justification hereafter. The man of faith is committed to certain expectations which the sceptic rejects. These are the specifically Christian eschatological expectations. Although these cannot be tested here, it is possible to indicate how they will be confirmed in the hereafter if Christian claims about it are true. So the content of faith is verifiable, though

17

not in a manner which removes its optional character here and now.

This is a remarkably balanced and resourceful combination of neo-orthodox theology and philosophical analysis. I shall first summarise it a little more formally, and then compare it with the Thomistic account of faith.

1. *Faith is not a form of assent to propositions, but a 'total interpretation' of experience.* Hick stresses, as many post-Kantian epistemologists have stressed, the interpretative element in all human experience. He points out that some philosophers have argued that an epistemological sceptic who refuses to interpret his experience in terms of our standard beliefs in a world of things and persons may be immune to decisive refutation; and that a moral sceptic who refuses to read his experience of the world as being informative of his moral obligations may be immune to such refutation also. He argues that the religious interpretation of the world as created by a God who offers a free personal relationship to his creatures represents a further step in an interpretative process which therefore can be questioned at earlier stages too. I shall not comment here on his epistemological claims about common-sense beliefs regarding the material world or about moral obligations. I merely point out here that if faith is interpreted in this way it clearly is a propositional activity. The propositions appear, as it were, within the response to experience, and the affirmation of them is what the act of faith in part consists of.

2. *Revelation is in the form of events and actions, not propositions.* While St Thomas is at pains to insist that the ultimate object of faith is God himself, not propositions about him, he clearly considers the revelation of God to take the form of pronouncements of propositions. To Hick, in the Protestant tradition, the propositions are the content of the interpretation of the revelation. The revelation is in the form of historical acts and events, which can be, and often are, interpreted in non-theistic ways. (They can also, of course, be interpreted in more theistic ways than one.) To interpret them in theistic ways is to accept and proclaim propositions about them. It is clear that although the combination of these views about faith and revelation allows far more doctrinal latitude, and far less rigorously literal reading of the

18

Scriptures, than the Thomistic view, it is nevertheless closer to it than it seems on the surface.

3. The interpretation of which faith consists can be understood in terms of 'seeing-as'. Wittgenstein, in the 'Philosophical Investigations', uses the example of ambiguous pictures, most famously Jastrow's duck-rabbit, as a clue to the understanding of our interpretation of our experience(13). Hick makes extended use of this illustration, stretching the meaning of it far beyond its original intent(14). It is characteristic of such experiences that they are induced in us by someone who is aware of both ways in which the pictures can be interpreted. One does not have to read the picture one way only. In the case of faith, however, it is clear that although it too is optional, Hick regards it, like St Thomas, as wholehearted.

4. Although faith is voluntary, it is rational. The purpose of Hick's epistemological analogies, his characterisation of faith as cognitive, and his emphasis on verifiability, is clearly to argue that faith, though optional is not irrational.

5. Its rationality is not, however, due to the possibility of prior demonstration of the existence of God. Apart from the failure of the traditional theistic proofs, Hick rejects the enterprise of natural theology as traditionally understood on the grounds that faith is voluntary and proofs would be coercive. Although faith is rational, unbelief is not irrational.

6. Faith and knowledge are not exclusive. Given the position outlined, it is clear that one can only insist that God exists within a context of faith. This being so, the claim that faith is a form of knowledge is a claim of faith and not a merely philosophical claim. Hick would, however, hold that the opposition of faith and knowledge is erroneous; that if God does exist, then the man of faith knows that he does, or at least can properly claim to. His argument that the content of faith is verifiable hereafter is not intended to suggest that in the hereafter we will have knowledge of something which is not a possible object of knowledge now. Its main purpose is to emphasise that some of Christianity's recent critics, who have suggested that its doctrines lack clear meaning because they are not subject to any procedure of verification, are mistaken.

I shall try at the end of this book to assess these two

19

positions about what faith is. It is important to notice at the outset that there are similarities between the positions, as well as dissimilarities. Both regard faith as including adherence to propositions. Both regard it as voluntary. Both regard it as rational. And both agree in holding that there is at least some tension between these latter two: that if faith is rational it is not rational in the strong sense that all of its content can be demonstrated; for if it could be, then faith would not be voluntary. This is the main reason why Hick rejects the enterprise of proving God's existence, and why St Thomas only allows natural theology a very limited sphere, and refuses to admit that one and the same person can have faith in a proposition and learn it from philosophical demonstration. I shall examine this shared doctrine as soon as possible. I shall take it for granted that God's existence has not been proved - not because this needs no argument, but because the arguments are to be found in abundance elsewhere. I shall rather examine the more general question of why this failure to prove God's existence has been argued by so many philosophers and theologians to be just what one would expect.

2 The Nature of Proof

(a) Proof from Premises and Proof without Premises

Many philosophers and theologians speak and write as though it has been established that one cannot prove the existence of God, or any propositions about God's nature or actions. In this Chapter and the next I shall examine this claim and some of its implications. In order to do this, I shall try to clarify in this Chapter what would be involved in a successful proof of God's existence, or, for that matter, a successful proof of any proposition. I shall then examine in the next Chapter some of the reasons there might be for holding that such an enterprise must fail. These reasons will include both philosophical and theological ones.

The enterprise of proving, or trying to prove, that God exists is often contrasted with that of convincing someone of his existence by an appeal to revelation, or to religious experience, or some other evangelistic means. But I do not wish to give an account of what a proof is that would rule out by fiat any claim that such appeals are proofs. It would be idle to deny that the concept of a proof (or the word 'proof') has more than one application (or more than one sense). I am concerned with clarifying the sense of the word 'proof' that is involved when the traditional arguments (the Ontological, the Cosmological, the Teleological) are referred to as proofs. This will clearly be the same sense that is involved when philosophers and theologians say that there can be no proof of God's existence. Since such a claim can be made, and often is made, in conjunction with an expressed intention to convince men of God by means of evangelistic appeals, an *a priori* refusal to let such means count as proofs would suggest a negative evaluation of them that it is no part of my purpose to make. On the other hand, it is essential so to define what a proof is that our definition allows us to preserve the distinction between the two modes of generating conviction of God. The only way of preserving it is to admit

21

that our definition covers only that sense of the word in which the contrast can be expressed (1).

The admission that a definition may fail to cover some quite legitimate uses of a word, however, must be made with care. In particular, we must bear in mind that those who have claimed to be able to prove God's existence have quite certainly held that they were showing their readers that God existed in a manner that was also suitable for showing men the truth of propositions of other kinds. We must try, therefore, to avoid the extreme particularism that would result if our definition of a proof were only appropriate to attempted proofs of statements with a theological subject-matter. In what follows I shall try to give an account of a common, indeed standard, understanding of what a proof is. That the word 'proof' is used at times in other ways I do not deny; indeed it must be emphasised. It is essential to my argument, however, that the use I do attempt to describe is not confined to proofs of propositions that are of religious interest.

I begin with the observation that we shall be considering proofs that involve processes of reasoning. It is quite proper to speak of proving to a sceptical grandfather that his grandson is four feet tall by pointing the boy out; or proving that the wine is all gone by producing the empty bottle. Fundamental epistemological issues are raised if we asked what is involved in proving something in such ways, but these are not our concern here. For, to put the matter very roughly, these are examples of proving something to someone by showing it to him, or getting him to observe it. In such cases it is out of place to speak of proving some conclusion to him *from premisses*. I am concerned with cases where proving something does proceed in this latter way: with ratiocinative proofs. It seems appropriate to put the distinction by saying that I shall be attempting to define indirect, rather than direct, proof.

(b) Moore on Proof from Premisses

There is surprisingly little philosophical literature on the nature of indirect proofs, especially when one reflects on how many attempted indirect proofs there are in philosophy.

22

One very valuable (and wholly non-theological) discussion of this question is to be found in the closing sections of G. E. Moore's famous lecture 'Proof of an External World' (2). In these sections Moore examines the question of what a proof is in order to answer those philosophers who feel that what he has offered as a proof of an external world is not a proof at all. My concern here is with the general concept of proof that Moore expresses, not with the question of how far he has been successful with his proof; but a few general comments on the argument of his lecture are still necessary.

Those without much recent acquaintance with his text are apt to say that Moore tried to prove the existence of an external world by raising his hand in the air. Needless to say, this is too simple. The structure of Moore's whole argument is this. He begins by quoting a statement from the preface to the second edition of Kant's 'Critique of Pure Reason', in which Kant says it is a scandal to philosophy that there is still need of a satisfactory proof of 'the existence of things outside of us'. He then sets out to discuss what sort of proof, if any, can be had of this. A great deal of Moore's lecture is concerned with revealing the ambiguities and complexities of the phrase 'things outside of us', and the related phrases 'things to be met with in space', and 'things external to our minds', and his discussion of these very difficult expressions remains a model of clarity and penetration. Its details do not, however, matter here. He claims that if he can prove that there are at least two things to be met with in space he will have proved that there are at least two things outside of us; and that he will have proved the former if he can prove that there exist, for example, a shoe and a sock, or a piece of paper and a human hand, or two shoes or two pieces of paper or two human hands. In other words, if he can prove that (for example) there are two human hands, this will in turn prove that there are at least two things to be met with in space, and this in turn will prove that there are at least two things outside of us. He speaks, therefore, of proving one thing in order to prove another, of one proof as a necessary preliminary to another. But the first stage in Moore's sequence of proofs (which is what *the* Proof of an External World now becomes) is a proof that there are two human hands. (He stresses that there are innumerable other pairs of things that he could prove the existence of, and therefore innumerable routes towards proving an external world.) It is in connection with the proof that two human hands exist that Moore's famous gesture comes in:

> 'I can prove now, for instance, that two human hands exist. How? By holding up my two hands, and saying, as I make a certain gesture with the right hand, 'Here is one hand', and adding, as I make a certain gesture with the left, 'and here is another'. (3)

He then goes on to discuss the obvious question of whether he has 'just now' proved that two human hands were then in existence. While in some of the remaining pages he does not always distinguish sharply between proving this and proving the existence of things outside of us, it is in general clear that the latter is proved by proving the former, not in the sense that they are proofs of the same proposition, but that the proof of two human hands gives us the necessary knowledge to generate a proof of things outside of us - at least as Moore sees the matter. Hence in outlining the conditions of satisfactory proof Moore concentrates on the question of whether or not he has managed to prove the proposition about two human hands. For simplicity it is this that I shall concentrate upon.

He insists that he has not proved the premises of his proof. He has not proved, that is, the two statements 'Here is one hand', and 'Here is another hand'. He insists nevertheless that his hearers, because they saw him raise each hand as he uttered these sentences, know these two premises to be true. Whether Moore is right in holding that they know this, or whether his opponents would be right in insisting that they would only know things of this sort if they were proved, rather than just shown, to be the case, does not concern us here. What is important is (a) that Moore is clearly speaking of the conditions for a satisfactory indirect proof (since if it is in order to speak of direct proofs, then proving one's hand exists by raising it looks like a very strong candidate), and (b) he is claiming that in an indirect proof the premises have to be known, though not necessarily proved (4). We are now in the midst of the conditions for proof in general, which Moore spells out in two very interesting paragraphs (5).

(c) Conditions for Successful Proof

Moore lists three conditions for a successful proof. One of them is clearly a double condition, and I shall divide it, speaking in consequence of four conditions. He speaks in this section of his lecture as though his argument has one conjunctive premiss ('Here is one hand, and here is another') and gives as its conclusion 'Two human hands exist at this moment'. Where I follow him in speaking of 'the premiss' it must be remembered that there may of course be two or more premisses in a proof.

(i) Moore's first condition is that in a satisfactory proof the premiss must be 'different from' the conclusion it is adduced to prove. (ii) His second condition is that the premiss must be true. (iii) His third condition is that the premiss has to be known to be true by the person offering the proof. (iv) His fourth condition is that the conclusion must follow from the premisses. I am not concerned to decide how far Moore's conditions are satisfied by his own argument, but only with the question of the adequacy of these conditions for determining what is a satisfactory indirect proof. Let us take them in turn.

(i) *Moore's first condition: that the premiss must be different from the conclusion.* At first sight this condition looks obvious, though it is also obvious that problems would arise when one tried to decide in particular cases whether or not it was satisfied. Because of this difficulty the condition needs to be stated with more care. We should begin by brushing aside any suggestion that if one statement follows from another it is somehow contained in it, and is therefore not different from it; for such a view would rule out all deductive proofs, in which conclusions follow from premisses, and would make Moore's first and fourth conditions incompatible with one another.

Moore does expand this first condition, in an unsatisfying but instructive way. His premiss, once again, is 'Here is one hand and here is another', and his conclusion is 'Two human hands exist'. He says these are different, because the

25

conclusion says less then the premiss does, and could be true even if the premiss were false. This suggests the following specification of this first condition: that the condition is violated only when the conclusion entails the premiss. We would feel uncomfortable, I think, in making what seems an obviously necessary condition quite as permissive as this. On the other hand, it does have to be made rather more permissive than some philosophers would like it to be. We must remember that not all bad proofs have to be ruled out by one of the conditions, as long as every bad proof is ruled out by their combination.

Consider the following example:

> God exists and created the world.
> Therefore, God exists.

As Moore sems to define the first condition this argument satisfies it, since the conclusion says less than the premiss, and does not entail it. Yet there is surely an inclination to say that the conclusion is not sufficiently 'different' from the premiss for the proof to be acceptable. One way of trying to express this might be to point out that no one could know the premiss to be true without already knowing that the conclusion was. While this seems indisputable, considerations about the knowledge needed for successful proof belong in the evaluation of Moore's third condition, and are best avoided here. And the difference Moore is concerned with seems in any case to be a difference that lies in the statements that go to make up the proof, rather than in the knowledge their user and hearer might have. I suggest, therefore, an alternative specification of Moore's first condition that would rule out the above argument, without ruling our Moore's proof. I suggest we say that in a successful proof one must not have to state the conclusion in order to state the premiss. In my example the premiss is a conjunctive statement, and one cannot state the conjunction without stating each part; since the conclusion is identical with one of the parts, one cannot state the premiss without stating it. In Moore's proof, although the premiss is a conjunction, the conclusion is not one of the parts of it. So Moore's proof meets the condition as I have specified it, and my example does not.

My version of Moore's first condition, however, is still quite permissive. It would allow the following argument, which could in fact pass as a degenerate version of the Cosmological Proof:

> Either nothing exists or God exists.
> Something exists (e.g. myself).
> Therefore, God exists.

Even though the first of the two premisses does, in a sense, contain the conclusion, it does not contain it in a way which makes the total argument violate my restatement of Moore's first condition. For the first premiss only contains the *words* 'God exists'. It is not the case that someone who stated the first premiss would thereby have stated that God exists. While it is true that someone who makes a statement of the form 'p and q' thereby states that p and states that q, it is not true that someone who makes a statement of the form 'not-p or q' has thereby stated p, or stated q. There may be grounds for rejecting the above argument, but they must be sought in one of the other of the conditions for proof.

I must, once again, emphasise that the first condition is not violated if one cannot state the premisses of an argument without making a statement which entails the conclusion. For such a situation would in fact be partially paradigmatic of a successful deductive proof.

With these provisos, we may accept Moore's first condition.

(ii) *Moore's second condition: that the premiss must be true.* This seems most obvious of all, and I shall not linger on it. One can, of course, derive true conclusions from false premisses by valid steps; but if a conclusion is reached in this way, it is not proved. The person who reaches it may have succeeded in proving it to his satisfaction. But proving something to one's own satisfaction is not proving it, it is merely thinking one has proved it; and one cannot even think one has proved it if one does not think that the premiss from which one has inferred it is true.

There is one possible kind of counter-example here. This is

the case of *reductio ad absurdum* proofs. These are arguments where someone shows a proposition, p, to be true by showing that its denial either is or entails a contradiction, or entails a known falsehood. It might very well seem that in these cases the proof has, in an obvious way, no premiss at all. Where we have a case in which the denial of p leads to a known falsehood merely, I incline to say that the contradictory of the known falsehood is a premiss in the argument, and is true. But where the denial of p leads to contradictions, I am more inclined to accept that there is no premiss and amend my account of the second condition to allow for this. Amended in the required way, it would read as follows: a successful proof, thus far, is an argument in which the conclusion derives either from premisses which are true, or is shown to have a contradictory which leads to contradictions. What I subsequently say about proof will, I think, still hold with this condition added - except, of course, that what I say about the relationships between premiss and conclusion will not apply. I shall assume no special difficulty to exist in cases where *reductio* arguments occur as stages in complex proofs that begin with true premisses.

(iii) *Moore's third condition: that the premiss must be known to be true.* There are temptations both to accept and to reject this condition. To decide between them is in effect to decide how far proof is 'person-relative' (6). It is to decide whether to think of proofs as sets of propositions with logical relationships between them, which satisfy the standards of proof whether anyone knows them or not, or to think of proof as an act which someone performs, and which requires for its performance a speaker and hearer. I do not wish to suggest that either way is wrong, or that in choosing to define what a proof is in one way precludes there being a perfectly consistent way of defining it in the other. I do not even, in our present context, wish to investigate whether, if there are two such compatible uses, one would have to be regarded as parasitic on the other. The former way of delineating what proof is is most tempting if we concentrate our attention on mathematical proofs, or demonstrations in formal logic, where the elements connected are formulae, and the relationship between these and the human activity of statement-making seems very distant (7). The latter way is clearly preferable when the units connected in the proof are (as our discussion of the first condition of proof has indicated) statements, and where the need is to determine the sense of proof which we have in mind when speaking, *inter alia,* of the theistic proofs. I would therefore recommend this second way. It would be convenient, nevertheless, to have some ground to offer for this preference other than its convenience for dealing with the kind of proof we wish to consider. I would like to borrow here a pair of arguments invented by George Mavrodes (8):

I. If there are intelligent beings living on the planet Mars, then the human race is not unique in the possession of rationality. There are intelligent beings living on the planet Mars. Therefore, the human race is not unique in the possession of rationality.

II. If there are no intelligent beings inhabiting the planet Mars, then there is no possibility of our achieving an interchange of rational ideas with that planet. There are no intelligent beings inhabiting the planet Mars. Therefore, there is no possibility of our achieving an interchange of rational ideas with that planet.

Now the conclusion of I is compatible with the conclusion of II. Both can be true. But on the basis of the criteria for successful proof that we have so far accepted, it is impossible to hold that both can be proved. For the second premiss of the first is incompatible with the second premiss of the second, so one of the arguments must have a false premiss, thus violating our second condition. If, however, we do not add the third condition about the need for the truth of the premisses to be known, we get the result that one of these two arguments already is a good proof. We just do not, inconveniently, know which one it is. So in constructing these two arguments we have proved one of the conclusions, but we cannot say which. This is not an absurd or intolerable result. But it is clearly more in accord with the most common use of the notion of proof to say that neither argument is a successful proof, because we do not know which one has true premisses. So I would recommend adding Moore's third condition: that the truth of the premiss or premisses must be known. In this we are adopting the use of 'proof' in which a proof is an act performed by making statements which serve as premises and which have to be known to be true for the proof to succeed. Proof in this sense has to be done by someone to someone, although of course in some instances the speaker and the hearer may be the same person. I would hold that this use of 'proof' is not invented, but actual and common.

Before proceeding to Moore's fourth condition, I must comment at some length on some very critical questions raised by the acceptance of the third. (a) If the premises have to be known to be true, is it necessary that the conclusion not be known? Can one, that is, prove something, or have something proved to one, if one knows it already? (b) Granted that proof requires knowledge, must proof yield knowledge? If something is proved to someone, does it follow that he then knows it? (c) Who has to know the truth of the premises or conclusion - the speaker, the hearer, or both?

(a) There is no doubt that some of the thinkers who have attempted to prove the existence of God have thought they knew God existed before they produced their arguments. There is no reason to doubt that the same belief regarding their conclusions has obtained among many people who have set out to prove things. If one made it a necessary condition of their having succeeded in proving them that they should not have known them first, one would have to determine independently whether the inventor of an argument knew the truth of its conclusion before deciding whether or not his invention was successful. This is clearly intolerable, partly because we may never be in a position to determine this, and partly because someone's knowing a truth of which he wishes to convince others is a prime reason for his trying to prove it to them. Of course, if someone already knows, or thinks he knows, that p, then in trying to prove that p he is not trying to learn that p is true; he already has learned this. But, leaving aside the needs of his hearers, he might still have reason to want to prove it for his own benefit - to prove it to himself, or at least for himself. He might, quite reasonably, want to reinforce his previous knowledge. He might want to see the interrelationships between different things that he knows. He might want to deepen his understanding of what

30

he already knows. There seems no reason, therefore, to suggest that proving that p is either impossible or pointless if the speaker already knows that p, even if the speaker and the hearer are identical. Suppose that they are not? Is it impossible that A should prove that p to B if B already knows that p? I feel some uncertainty here. A can certainly tell B that p even if B already knows it. He cannot inform him that p if he already knows it. Is proving like telling in this respect, or like informing? I think it is clear that the normal occasions for speaking of A's proving that p to B would be occasions where B was either ignorant or sceptical, or at best merely inclined towards p without conviction. In each of these cases A could sensibly try to prove that p to B. But does this show that A could not prove that p to B if B already knew it, or merely that there would be no point in his doing so? I am unsure here, but I do not think a decision on this is required. For even though B might know that p, it seems clear that there could be the same point in A's proving that p as there might be if A is proving that p for his own benefit. So even if B's knowing that p already is sufficient to make it logically impossible for A to prove it to him, it does not make it logically impossible for A to prove it for him (9). B might, through having it proved to or for him, come to have his previous knowledge of it reinforced, or to see its relationship to other things that he also knows, or to have his understanding of it deepened. So proving it to or for B is not something that there would be no reason to do, merely because B already knows it. So although proof is person-relative, it can be done even though the person proving, or the person proved to, or both, know the truth of the conclusion already.

This is a matter on which confusion can easily arise, because of general theses about the relationship of knowledge to faith. St Thomas, as we have seen, would hold that a person cannot both know that p, and hold that p on faith. So if someone holds that p on faith, and p is then proved to him through the resources of natural theology, his faith is on this view replaced by knowledge. It is not reinforced by knowledge, at least as far as p is concerned, though his faith in the truth of q or r may of course be reinforced by his newly-acquired knowledge that p. Suppose, however,

31

someone were to deny that faith and knowledge are exclusive in this way, or even hold, as Hick would seem to, that faith is a form of knowledge? In such a case, the fact that someone knew that p and the fact that p was one of the things he held on faith would not be incompatible. If such a person then had p proved to or for him, his faith could be reinforced by this, not replaced by it.

So anyone who holds, with St Thomas, that no man can hold on faith something that has been proved to him, or can have something proved to him and hold it on faith, must rest his case for this upon an independent attempt to show that faith and knowledge are incompatible.

The influence of St Thomas upon our whole understanding of the nature and purpose of proofs of God may make us overlook the fact that there is at least one very significant precedent for the view that one can know that God exists, that such knowledge can be a matter of faith, and that a proof of God's existence can still serve to reinforce that faith by increasing one's understanding. The precedent of course is the case of St Anselm. No one reading the 'Proslogion' can possibly imagine that St Anselm does not think he knows that God exists before he starts; or that the document is not a classic expression of faith; or that it is not an attempt to prove God's existence! He considers himself to have faith and to be seeking understanding; but it would be very dubious exegesis to hold that this has to be a case of faith trying to replace itself by something else. Of course Anselm's account of what he is about may be incoherent; but it is not obviously so, and his critics among philosophers have wisely concentrated their efforts upon uncovering weaknesses in the Ontological Proof, not upon questioning the authenticity of its setting (10).

No philosopher ought to find it odd that anyone would try to prove something that he already knows. For the three centuries from Descartes to Moore, this sort of activity has been one of philosophy's major preoccupations.

(b) Must proof result in knowledge? If a conclusion is successfully proved to someone, does it follow from this that he knows it? It is very natural to assume that it does. Surely, if A proves that p to B, by starting from premisses that B

32

knows to be true, and proceeding by valid steps to p, and B can see that these steps are valid ones, and yet B does not clearly appear now to know that p, B must be lying? Unfortunately not. There might be cases where these conditions were satisfied and yet it was still uncertain whether or not B knew that p. He might not accept it. He might, for example, have an ingrained tendency of long standing to believe p to be false. Its being now proved to him will set up a conflict between this tendency and his new tendency to behave as though p is true. He will oscillate, so that we shall be unclear whether he knows p or not. Such a person is acting irrationally; but people do do this. Alternatively, B might know the truth of the premises and see that they lead to p, but find p so unpalatable that he cannot admit it either to us or to himself. He may, in other words, deceive himself with regard to p. In cases like this it is clear that the proof ought to result in knowledge on the part of the hearer, but it is not clear that it has done so. What we tend to say about someone in this position is not that he knows that p, but that he knows it *very well,* and knowing something very well is, paradoxically, less than knowing it. I submit that in these cases, where a hearer behaves irrationally with regard to the conclusion of a proof, or deceives himself with regard to its truth, and yet knows the truth of the premises and can see the validity of the inferences, the conclusion has been proved to him even though it is not clear that he knows that it is true. Conversely, I would submit that where a conclusion has thus been proved to someone, yet he still does not clearly know it, he must be guilty of irrationality or self-deception with regard to it.

It is very natural for a philosopher to want to say that where someone does not clearly satisfy the criteria for knowing the conclusion of a proof, this must be because he does not know the premises to be true, or does not understand that they entail the conclusion, or is just dissembling the knowledge he has. Not knowing must, on this view, either be due to ignorance or foolishness, or be a pretence. But such a stance pays too high a compliment to human consistency. For the notion of self-deception does have application; and this is one of the places where it has it (11). It has application where it is just too easy to speak of ignorance or hypocrisy; and to speak of foolishness is especially implausible, because clever people are better at deceiving themselves than stupid people are. It is often hard to distinguish self-deception from hypocrisy or ignorance, and this notoriously makes the concept of self-deception very difficult to analyse, since analyses tend very readily to lead to paradoxes. But self-deception does occur: more correctly, it is done. And the reason that analyses of it tend to lead to paradoxes is that self-deception is a manifestation of a conflict-state: one in which men have a strong motive to believe the opposite of that to which the evidence directs them. In so far as they are successful in doing it, they will seem not to know that which the evidence points to; in so far as they have some need to do it, they will give some signs that suggest they know it nevertheless. Self-deception has many mechanisms. One that should be familiar enough to philosophers is mentioned (though it is not called this) by J. F. Ross:

> Yet the more *expensive*, emotionally or intellectually, the hypothesis that God exists (or any other hypothesis for that matter) is for a man, the less likely he is to be convinced by a sound argument for it. For consider a sound argument of the form: a, b, therefore c. If a man for whom c is extremely expensive (i.e. who thinks belief in c would require a mssive alteration in his conceptual scheme and his way of life) sees that given what he already claims to know (and in fact does know), both a and b must be considered true and entail c, he will very probably abandon some of his former claims to know (and in doing so, end by knowing *less* than he did before) in order to avoid accepting the conclusion he dislikes and whose falsity he has privileged as more evident than his beliefs, a and b. (12).

The manoeuvre that Ross describes is very familiar, It closely resembles one which is often desirable in philosophy, namely that of questioning some set of assumptions when it is seen where they lead. A classic example of such a move is to be found in one of G. E. Moore's recommendations. In his essay 'Hume's Philosophy', he outlines three increasingly sceptical

34

positions taken up by Hume concerning the extent of human knowledge (13). The second of these is the view that we cannot know any external facts, and on Moore's account of him, Hume infers this sceptical result from two general epistemological principles which seem far more attractive than the result Hume derives from them. Moore simply recommends that, contrary to the common practice, a reader of Hume should recognise the fact (if it is one) that these principles lead to this result as sufficient to show it to have been a mistake to accept them. It is far more plausible to insist that we do know some external facts than to rest satisfied with any principle which turns out on examination to make this questionable. Moore's determination to turn sceptical arguments back upon themselves in this way has been enormously beneficial in twentieth-century philosophy. It is clear from this one example that philosophers should never assume too readily that they know that the premisses of such arguments are true. The same applies, without doubt, to arguments for the existence of God. But whatever the subject-matter, there is a genuine distinction between being properly on guard against agreeing too readily that one knows the premisses of an attempted proof to be true, whether its conclusion would be welcome or not, and being prepared even to put into question propositions that one does know to be true when the conclusion drawn from them is an unwelcome one. The latter move is a perversion of the former. Where the premisses of an argument are not known but mistakenly taken to be, an attempted reversal of the argument is a sign of professional acumen. Where the premisses are known, but are then said not to be, because of the unwelcome nature of their results, such a reversal is a case of self-deception (14). I do not suggest it is at all easy to say which is happening, or even that it is always seemly to offer a suggestion! Nor, of course, do I suggest that this is the only way in which someone who knows the premisses of an argument to be true and can see the validity of the steps can fail clearly to know the conclusion to be true: it is merely one familiar way, and a way where the mechanisms of self-deception are on the surface.

(c) I turn finally to the question of who has to know the

35

truth of the premisses or conclusion for there to be a proof. This can be dealt with quite briefly. It seems clear from the preceding that the hearer of a successful proof must know the truth of the premisses, though he may not clearly know the truth of the conclusion. If he does not know this, however, this must be due to irrationality or self-deception on his part. As far as the speaker is concerned (and here we are of course dealing with those cases where the two are not identical), a decision on how much he has to know depends on whether or not we wish to say that someone could prove something by accident. I do not see why we should not admit this to be possible. It is surely possible that some professor of philosophy has by this time made some statements in class and drawn a conclusion from them, intending this to be merely an example and not considering himself or anyone else to know the statements to be true, and yet one of his audience has known them to be true, has seen that the conclusion follows, and has thereby had a proposition proved to him by accident. In such a case I do not see why we should not agree that there has been a proof performed. Given, however, that we are speaking of proof as something someone does to someone, we cannot go on to admit that in such a case there has been a proof where no such person is in the audience.

Cases of accidental proof would have to be rare ones; but we are speaking here solely of logical possibilities. If we admit that such a case is logically possible, and combine this admission with the considerations I have offered under (b) above, we reach the result that it is also logically possible that there might be cases where there has been a proof, and yet neither the speaker nor the hearer end up knowing the truth of the conclusion (even though the hearer must know the truth of the premisses). This is not a paradoxical result: for on the account of proof I am offering it is still true that when our conditions are satisfied the hearer *ought,* given his other knowledge, to know the truth of the conclusion when the argument is over. Another result of our discussion is to allow us to accommodate those occasions where we say something has been proved true by events. Such an idiom suggests that we do not need to have a speaker, someone who offers the proof or does the proving, at all. It does not seem to me to matter whether we say, in such cases, that we have a proof because the hearer recognises the events (such recognition amounting here to his knowledge of the truth of the premises of a proof), sees where they point and thereby comes to know the truth of the conclusion or irrationally refuses to; or say that in such cases one and the same person serves both as speaker and hearer, formulating the premises and conclusion in one capacity and responding to them in another. (What our account of proof would not permit is saying that events have proved something when no one is in a position to recognise this. That it is in order on occasions to say this suggests the existence of some other sense of 'prove' in which it can be said.)

(iv) *Moore's fourth condition: that the conclusion must follow from the premises*. It is important to decide on the necessity of this condition when considering the possibility of proofs of the existence of God, because of the importance in the history of the theistic proofs of probability arguments. The most important case is the Argument from Design. It is not usually presented in a deductive form, in which the conclusion is alleged to follow on pain of self-contradiction from the premises. There is no doubt that we sometimes use the word 'proof' in such a way that proof is restricted to cases where the conclusion follows in this manner. It may be that the non-deductive nature of the Design Argument is the reason why it is customary to refer to it as the Design *Argument*, and why it is commoner to talk of the Ontological and Cosmological *Proofs*. But there is at most a tendency to make this distinction between these three in this manner - the Argument from Design is, in one version, the Teleological *Proof*. It seems foolish, in view of the importance of this argument in the history of natural theology, not to adopt an account of proof which will allow us at least to consider this famous argument as an attempted proof. One way, which would preserve the wholly deductive character of proof, would be to insist on dressing up all versions of the Design Argument in a deductive form. One such version would then be:

Order is always the result of design.
There is order throughout the universe.
Therefore, the universe is the result of design.

Most would agree, however, that this is a rather misleading formulation of a line of thought which is less misleadingly presented like this:

Order is found over and over again to be the result of design.
There is order throughout the universe.
So there is very probably a Designer of the universe.

There are also many other arguments (such as that from moral experience, or from the consensus of mankind) which only purport to show that the conclusion that God exists is rendered probable by the evidence adduced in the premisses. We do, however, need to preserve a clear distinction between proving something and showing it to be likely. What we need to do is to maintain this distinction without insisting that in the former case the relationship between premisses and conclusion has to be deductive. If we can do this, we shall then be able to say, as we surely will want to say, that some of the theistic arguments that are non-deductive (e.g. the Argument from Design in its best-known versions) are purported proofs, whereas some of them are not thought even by their proponents as doing more than rendering God's existence fairly probable or likely.

The only way of managing this is by leaning on the notion of degrees of probability or likelihood, and claiming that a successful proof is one which shows its conclusion to have the highest possible degree of this. This we may call overwhelming probability or likelihood. While this is a notion which may well defy definition, it is entirely familiar. It can be connected with the concept of rationality in the following way. We would not be inclined to say that someone who agreed that the premisses of an argument rendered its conclusion likely or probable, but still rejected that conclusion, was responding irrationally. This would be far too strong an adverb to apply to his refusal. On the other hand, this is what we would be likely to say of someone who rejected the conclusion of an argument in which he could see the premisses rendered the conclusion overwhelmingly probable.

I propose, therefore, to allow as successful proofs not only arguments in which a conclusion is shown to be true by means of premisses which are known to be true and from which it deductively follows, but also arguments in which a conclusion is shown to be true by means of premisses which are known to be true and which render it overwhelmingly probable. In these latter cases someone who knows the premisses to be true and can see that they make the conclusion overwhelmingly probable but still rejects it, is behaving irrationally or deceiving himself.

It seems to me that Cleanthes, in Hume's 'Dialogues on Natural Religion', considers that the facts or order and adjustment in the natural world make God's existence overwhelmingly probable in this way; and that Philo's arguments against Cleanthes are intended to show that they do not make it overwhelmingly probable. It would thus seem to be ground common to both sides that if they did render God's existence overwhelmingly probable, his existence would have been proved by Cleanthes. (This is not inconsistent with Hume's dogma that no matter of fact can be proved *a priori*. For that is not the same as a doctrine that no matter of fact can be proved. Hume feels the need to show that this particular matter of fact is not susceptible of proof by examining the strength of the evidence offered, which he would not need to do, on his doctrines, in the case of *a priori* proofs - the Ontological and Cosmological arguments are dismissed in one paragraph (15).)

Having examined Moore's suggested conditions for a successful proof, I can now offer a summary account of what a proof is. I suggest we have a successful indirect proof of a conclusion from premisses when the premisses can be stated without stating the conclusion; when the premisses are true; when they are known by the hearer to be true; when the conclusion either follows from them or is rendered overwhelmingly probable by them; and when the hearer can see that it is. I would suggest that we have a successful indirect proof of a conclusion without premisses when the conclusion has a contradictory which entails a contradiction, and when the hearer knows that that statement is a contradiction and can see that the contradictory of the conclusion entails it. If these conditions are satisfied, then the conclusion has been proved. It is not also necessary that the hearer should be ignorant of the truth of the conclusion beforehand, or that he should clearly know the truth of the conclusion afterwards. If he does not clearly know it afterwards, however, this must be because of irrationality or self-deception on his part.

I shall proceed on the assumption that the traditional proofs of God's existence have been attempts to satisfy these condtions. I will also proceed on the assumption that they have all failed to satisfy at least one of them. I cannot justify either of these assumptions here. For the latter assumption, I must lean on the very extensive literature that deals with the merits and defects of the traditional arguments. Regarding the former one, it is perhaps sufficient to claim that if they have failed to meet these conditions they have not been successful proofs in the sense I have defined, and that this sense is close enough to the ones used in discussions I shall subsequently refer to for my comments on these discussions to be apposite.

3 Not being Able to Prove the Existence of God

(a) Why Proving God's Existence Might be Impossible

Given the preceding account of what a proof would be, what are we to make of the common claim that one cannot prove the existence of God? I shall begin by considering some philosophical reasons that might be offered in favour of this opinion.

If our previous account of proof is correct, someone who knew it to be impossible to prove the existence of God would have to know either (a) that there are no true statements from which God's existence would follow, or which would render God's existence overwhelmingly probable; or (b) that if there are such statements no one can know them to be true; or (c) that even if there are such statements and someone can know them to be true, no one can see that God's existence follows from them or is rendered overwhelmingly probable by them. To know any one of these things is to know a great deal. How would anyone come to know any of these things? One way would be by proving one of them; but how would one do this? One possible way of proving that one cannot prove that God exists would be to prove that God does not exist. There are at least two possible ways of attempting such a proof. One is to try to show that the statement that God exists entails contradictions. The other is to try to find some premiss, known to be true, from which God's non-existence follows. The first way has been tried by J. N. Findlay, in his 'Ontological Disproof' of the existence of God (1). The second way has been tried by all those who have contended that the statement 'There is evil' is inconsistent with traditional doctrines of God as creator (2). I do not think that either attempt has succeeded. I can only state this opinion here, however, and not argue for it, just as I was not able to offer reasons for rejecting the traditional proofs that God does exist (3).

It is common for claims like the claim that it is impossible to prove the existence of God to be inferred by philosophers from general epistemological principles, the strength of which it is impossible to examine here. But such a method is bound to suffer from the defect that it is always open to someone else to claim that the likelihood of such principles being sound ones is no greater than the countervailing likelihood of the enterprise which they exclude being possible. To refute such a counter-claim one would have to give very strong independent justification of the principles to which one appeals. To take a crude case, it used to be fashionable to say, or imply, that proving God's existence would be metaphysics, and metaphysics is impossible. The burden of showing this vast claim to be true has not, as far as I can see, been discharged by anyone, or even very clearly understood by anyone. A slightly subtler argument is to be found in Hume, who tells us that no matter of fact can be proved *a priori*. He sees clearly, of course, that only some attempted proofs of God's existence are ruled out by this principle (hence the lengthy examination of the Argument from Design in the 'Dialogues'); but even if we confine our attention to those arguments which are ruled out by it, we quickly face the fact that the principle itself is merely inferred from Hume's previous doctrine that 'all the objects of human reason or enquiry' can be divided into relations of ideas and matters of fact - and this doctrine, notoriously, he merely *states* (4). While it is hardly plausible to say that Kant, in the 'Critique of Pure Reason', did not offer independent arguments for his view that reason should confine itself to matters of possible experience, it is noteworthy that in the Dialectic he does not confine himself to inferring the futility of philosophical speculations that transgress this restriction, but uncovers, in great detail, the confusions which such speculations in fact contain, most notably the defects in the traditional attempts to prove the existence of God.

The moral to be drawn is that the confidence with which many philosophers are prone to assert that proof of God's existence is impossible is probably not matched by the possession of solid arguments, since the assertion is the expression of a very broad claim indeed. There is certainly no sufficient ground for refusing to examine on their own merits any future proofs of God's existence that are offered. In so far as philosophical scepticism about the possibility of theistic proofs has a basis at all, it is usually the result of the failure of the proofs that philosophers have encountered. The failure of attempts to prove God's existence is clearly inadequate to supply us with a proof that God's existence cannot ever be proved. If it supports any conclusion at all, however, it is a sceptical one. It is often necessary, even in such a ratiocinative discipline as philosophy, to proceed on grounds which one is not in a position to establish. It is not only sometimes necessary, but it can be done with minimal risk, if one is aware that the grounds are not established. The common scepticism about the possibility of proving God's existence is a scepticism which I share, and upon which I shall build as the argument of the book proceeds - after attempting to give somewhat clearer definition to it. But I do not offer in its favour anything more conclusive than the revelations of the defects in the traditional arguments that we owe to Hume and Kant and their critical successors. Indeed, I would urge that our scepticism about the chances of proofs for God's existence should be matched by a parallel scepticism about the chances of proving, rather than expecting, that there cannot be any.

At this point, however, we must turn to consider at least some of the theological reasons that have been offered for the view that the attempt to prove God's existence is doomed to failure. Such reasons are often based upon statements about the nature of Good, or about man's relationship (or lack of relationship) to God, being such as to preclude successful proof. They would therefore only serve to convince someone who believed that God does exist and has the nature alleged, and that man does have, or lack, such a relationship to him. My argument cannot presuppose such beliefs. But in spite of this, these theological considerations are of great importance. For one thing, if their being true, and being known to be, would suffice to prove that God's existence could not be proved, then no one who denies that God exists could reasonably use the failure of any attempted proof of his existence as an argument against theism. For such a failure would be something to be expected if theism were true. Similarly, if their being true, and being known to

43

be, would suffice to prove that God's existence could not be proved, then anyone who already thinks he knows that God exists and wishes to reinforce his knowledge, or make it available to others, by constructing a proof of God's existence, could learn from the strength of these theological considerations that what he was trying to do was impossible and likely to misrepresent the nature of God. I wish to suggest that some theological considerations that have been offered are not in fact sufficient for this; that even if they were true, and known to be true, they would not suffice to prove that God's existence could not be proved to men.

One such theological reason is the view that men are so sinful that their very thought-processes are perverted, so that knowledge of God can only come to them through divine grace and not through their own unaided efforts. In fact, attempts on the part of men to prove the existence of God and thus come to know of God without recourse to divine grace are a manifestation of pride. There are several replies to this. (i) Even if it were true that all attempts to prove God's existence were entered into from sinful motives, it would only follow that they were doomed to failure if it were added that God would not permit the success of any enterprise whose motives were not free of sin. It is hard to see how this could be added in any theological tradition without a great deal of argument. (ii) Even if it were agreed that no one who did not know of God beforehand could come to know of him by setting up a proof of his existence, it would not follow from this that no one could successfully set up such a proof. For those who have tried to prove God's existence have not always tried to do so in order to produce knowledge of God where it has not previously existed. Proof, as we have seen in our discussion of Moore's third condition, can have other purposes, including the reinforcement and deeper comprehension of previous knowledge. (iii) The very most that an argument like the one before us can show is that knowledge of God is impossible except through grace. But even if we do not question a dichotomy such as 'knowledge-through-proof versus knowledge-through-grace', this does not show that God's existence cannot be successfully proved. For someone can have something proved to him and yet, through irrationality or self-deception, not know it as a result. So

44

even if men cannot know of God save through grace, and grace does not operate through proofs, God's existence might still have been proved to them. Their sinfulness might prevent them recognising that it had.

Similar comments apply to the argument, sometimes encountered, that a proof of God's existence can merely result in the acceptance of the proposition that God exists; and that the result of conversion is not mere assent to a proposition but faith in God. If it is possible to have knowledge that God exists without having faith in God, then the fact (if it is one) that a man could not get faith through proof would not show that he could not acquire this knowledge through proof; and even if he could not get knowledge through proof this might not be because there are no successful proofs but because of defective responses to successful ones. If it is not possible to have knowledge that God exists without having faith in God, then the fact (if it is one) that a man cannot get faith through proof would indeed show that he could not get knowledge through proof either; but, for the same reason, this would not in turn show that successful proof was impossible. The objection we are considering applies in any case only if the sole purpose of proving God's existence is that of converting the hearer. But we have already seen that proof can have other functions, at least for those already converted.

A third theological consideration sometimes brought against the possibility of proving the existence of God is of greater importance. It is roughly as follows. A successful proof coerces acceptance of its conclusion. God, however, does not coerce his creatures into believing in him, but respects their freedom. He therefore would not permit successful proofs. I shall illustrate this argument by some lengthy quotations, because a proper assessment of it is very important. The first comes from Professor Alasdair MacIntyre.

> . . . suppose religion could be provided with a method of proof. Suppose, for example, as was suggested earlier, that the divine omnipotence was so manifest that whenever anyone denied a Christian doctrine he was at once struck dead by a thunderbolt. No doubt the conversion of

45

England would ensue with a rapidity undreamt of by the Anglican bishops. But since the Christian faith sees true religion only in a free decision made in faith and love, the religion would by this vindication be destroyed. For all the possibility of free choice would have been done away. Any objective justification of belief would have the same effect. Less impressive than thunderbolts, it would equally eliminate all possibility of a decision of faith. And with that, faith too would have been eliminated. (5)

The second is from Hick.

We must ask: why should God want to present himself to his human creatures in such an indirect and uncertain way instead of revealing himself in some quite unambiguous fashion that would permit no possible room for doubt as to his reality? Perhaps the answer is that God is leaving men free in relation to himself. Perhaps he has deliberately created an ambiguous world for us just in order that we shall *not* be compelled to be conscious of him. But why not? .... God, if he is known to exist, can only be known as the One who makes a total difference for us. For he is known as infinitely higher than us, in worth as well as in power, and as having so made us that our own final self-fulfilment and happiness are also the fulfilment of his purpose for us. I cannot know that such a Being exists and be at the same time indifferent to him. For in knowing him I know myself as created and dependent, a creature on the periphery of existence, whose highest good lies in relation to the divine centre of reality. And so if the man who comes to be conscious of God in this way is to remain a free and responsible personality, the knowledge of God must not be forced upon him, but on the contrary, it must depend upon his own willingness to live in the presence of a higher being whose very existence, when we are conscious of it, sets us under an absolute claim. (6)

Though neither of these passages refers explicitly to any of the traditional theistic proofs, it is clear from the immediately ensuing passages in MacIntyre, and from other passages in Hick's writings, that they do have this application.

And as we have understood what proof is, it is clear not only from MacIntyre but from Hick also, that whatever facts would be thought to put God's existence beyond reasonable doubt could serve as premises in successful proofs. We must put aside one obvious element in MacIntyre's example: the fact that if nay-sayers were struck down by thunderbolts everyone would be frightened into belief in God. Being frightened and being free are not simple opposites. It might very well be that an all-good God would not permit any proof of his existence that frightened men into believing in him. What is at issue is whether or not he could permit the existence of facts which proved his existence, where this is understood to mean merely that they entailed it or made it overwhelmingly probable, so that disbelief was thereby shown to be irrational. Proofs thus understood do not compel assent, as we have seen, because men are irrational and do deceive themselves; and Hick's statements show one reason why they might choose such courses rather than accept the conclusion of such proofs. In such cases, however, God's existence might have been proved to them nevertheless. What Hick refers to as men's 'cognitive freedom' (7) can be shown by their dressing up their refusal to accept what has been clearly shown in the form of specious counter-arguments. I am not of course arguing that the arguments brought by philosophers against the traditional proofs are specious; merely that the human capacity to create specious arguments in the face of successful proofs, and to allow themselves to be persuaded by them, is sufficient to show the possibility of both the existence of successful proofs on any subject-matter, God's existence included, and the freedom of men not to come to know the truth of their conclusions. Proof does not necessarily yield knowledge, for men can be irrational or deceive themselves, and as free agents they may do either. So God's existence might, for all this shows us, have been proved over and over again to men, and yet the only people not hindered by their own wilfulness from knowing that God exists might be those who had come to know this by some other means.

So the most that these theological objections could show is that the philosophical enterprise of trying to prove God's existence will not issue in knowledge of it if such knowledge

47

is not already present in some other way. This result would not be trivial, for it would suffice to make it clear that the evangelistic value of philosophic attempts would be low. This is important. But it is not a surprise. Someone who does not have knowledge of God but wishes to gain it if it can be gained, is no doubt best advised not to spend his time on natural theology. But this does not show that any one of the many attempted proofs found in the pages of natural theology is a failure. It only shows that if it is a success, such a person will miss this. On the other hand, if this in turn should seem worrying, it does not show that any one of these proofs is a success, or that any of the objections raised against it is unsound.

I would suggest, therefore, that one doctrine on which both of our two accounts of the nature of religious faith are agreed is mistaken. This is the doctrine that there is some necessary connection between the voluntary character of faith and the non-demonstrability of that which the man of faith believes. Even though both accounts include the claim that faith is a rational stance, both reject the suggestion that unbelief could be an irrational stance, at least with regard to some critical beliefs the man of faith has. If our examination of the nature of proof is sound, this rejection is unjustified. For proof does not compel assent; so the voluntariness of the assent involved in faith does not itself show that a man cannot hold on faith something that has been proved to him. Once this is seen, it becomes much harder to try to turn the absence of good proofs of God's existence to theological advantage. There may in fact be no proofs of God's existence or of any other proposition to which the man of faith is committed; and the failure of the attempted proofs is a reason to expect this to continue. But the voluntariness of faith, and any spiritual merit it may show, would not be put in jeopardy if there were such proofs. Admitting something one does not want to be true can still be good, and denying something one does not want to be true can still be evil, when what is admitted or denied has been proved.

In spite of the defects of these theological arguments, it is reasonable to hold that God's existence cannot be proved on the basis of the repeated failures of the attempts to prove it - even though it is not irrational not to hold it! Let us now

48

look at some of the consequences of holding it, in the light of the complex nature of the concept of proof. An examination of these consequences can lead to a deeper understanding than the philosophical literature often gives us of the nature of the gulf that separates those who have faith from those who do not.

(b) Two Kinds of Statement

Believers are not apt to state that God exists very often. They are far more likely to make statements about God's nature and his alleged dealings with men. This has led some misguided apologists to claim that there is some logical oddity about the statement that God exists (8). It is true that believers are less prone to state that God does exist than unbelievers are to state that he does not; for believers are users of religious language, and unbelievers are self-conscious abstainers from the use of it. Believers are more apt to make other sorts of statements about God than this one. But this does not show that in denying that God exists unbelievers are not denying something that believers believe; nor does it show that those who have tried to prove that God exists have not been trying to prove something that believers believe. No doubt in some cases their very attempt to prove it has been an attempt to support a statement that they have actually made in response to the unbelievers' denials. What it does show is that God's existence is something that is a necessary condition of the truth of the other things that believers say about God and his relationships to men, and that in telling us of these, believers proceed from the belief that God exists, without stating that belief in most cases. In order to proceed with our argument, we must now consider briefly the relationship between the statement that God exists and the many other statements that depend in this way upon it, such as the statement that God loves his creatures, that Jesus was the Son of God, that all men have sinned in the sight of God, or that God pardons all those who truly repent and unfeignedly believe his holy Gospel.

Unfortunately this is not so easy. In the first place it is not very illuminating to say that all the statements just alluded to are 'about God'. Although 'God loves his creatures' is no doubt about God, is 'All men have sinned in the sight of God' about God? Perhaps we might say that it is. But then, what about 'Jones believes in God'? Whatever tempts us to say that the former of these is about God is likely to tempt us in the latter case too, but in the latter case the statement would clearly still be true even if God does not exist, whereas neither of our first two examples could be true if God does not exist. So although we might be tempted to say that the statements that believers make (and unbelievers do not make) are about God, this does not seem to be enough to distinguish them, since the same thing could as easily be said about many of the statements that unbelievers make too. In addition to this, there are many statements that believers make which depend in the way we are trying to articulate on the existence of God, but which could be said to be about God only in the most strained sense; for example, 'Only the elect will attain salvation', or 'All men are sinners'. Neither of these contains the word 'God', yet both belong very clearly to the discourse of Christian theism and could not be stated with consistency by atheists.

A natural suggestion is that the statements in our original list, and these others also, are statements which depend for their truth on the truth of the statement that God exists (though not of course only upon this). This suggestion takes us into some well-known controversies in philosophical logic on which I would hope to avoid commitment in the present context as far as possible. Theists disagree among themselves about many things, for example over whether salvation will be vouchsafed to all men or only to some. An atheist faced with these two competing claims will of course deny them both, even though for the theist they exclude each other. The atheist might very well express his rejection by saying that both these competing claims are false. On the other hand, if he were fairly sophisticated in philosophical logic at least, he might say that since God does not exist, the question of the truth or falsity of either of these claims does not arise. To put it this way suggests, faintly paradoxically, that not only does the truth of each depend on the truth of the claim that God exists, but the falsity of each does also. In our present context I see no need to force a decision on which is the right way for him to talk, though both ways of speaking have reason on their side. We could say that the theist's statements are statements which depend for their truth on the truth of the statement that God exists, or we could say that they are statements which depend for their *truth or falsity* on the truth of the statement that God exists. To insist on the former is to obscure the special character of the atheist's rejection of theistic controversies; to insist on the latter is to ascribe more sophistication to his choice of words for expressing that rejection than seems plausible. So I shall try to avoid stating the relationship that concerns us in a way that requires a decision on this particular issue.

We are now in a position to reject another natural suggestion: that we try to define the relationship that concerns us in terms of the notion of entailment. We could not say that 'God exists' is entailed by 'Only the elect will attain salvation'. If one statement entails another, then somone who contradicts the second contradicts the first. But someone who contradicts 'God exists' does not contradict 'Only the elect will attain salvation'; to contradict this is to say something equivalent to 'Salvation is not confined to the elect', which the atheist cannot admit either. There is another, quite distinct obstacle. We have seen reason to emphasise the dangers of over-confidence about the impossibility of proving that God exists. If our commitment to this position were unjustified, it might be because someone was able to find a statement, or set of statements, which entailed that God existed. Certainly some attempted proofs have involved this claim. If they were to find such a statement, or such a set of statements, they would be likely to be statements which people had hitherto been unable to see entailed this conclusion; so much intermediate reasoning might be needed to show that the entailment was present. If we were to define the relationship that we are trying to characterise in terms of entailment, it would be a consequence of this that the premisses of such an imagined proof would have to be counted part of the religious discourse. This could not be held to be true for many of the premisses that have been offered in the past in attempted theistic proofs. While it might be that all the premisses that could generate such imagined proofs were in fact statements that are part of religious discourse, it would be foolish to

51

make this a matter of definition.

An alternative to the notion of entailment is Strawson's 'presupposition' (9). While this notion was originally introduced into philosophical logic in order to avoid the difficulties attending the use of the notion of entailment in contexts involving definite descriptions, it would be infelicitous here. To use it would be to say that the theist, in making the sorts of statement that are before us, presupposes that God exists, but does not, in making those statements, *say* that God exists. In religious contexts, however, the word 'presuppose' has very undesirable overtones. Presupposing is something one can do by casual, even frivolous, choice; even if the choice is neither casual nor frivolous, it is something one can do for the sake of an argument. ('Let us presuppose that . . .') It would be a caricature of theism to suggest that this is what theists do. Since one of our purposes is to throw light on the nature of the faith that believers have, it would be quite unsuitable to our objective to make use of a term with such misleading connotations.

In the light of these difficulties I shall introduce a distinction that I hope will capture the relationship that we have discussed, but avoid irrelevant controversies. It is the distinction between 'theistic and non-theistic statements'. I call a statement a theistic statement when, if it were true, it could only be known to be true by someone who knew that God exists. Any statement not in this category I call a non-theistic statement. I assert, therefore, a necessary connection between the knowledge of the truth of any statement I call theistic and the knowledge of the existence of God. Consequently anyone who denies there is such a necessary connection in a particular case, must, in my terminology, deny that the statement in question is a theistic one. I would hold, for example, that 'God loves the world' is theistic; that if anyone were to know this to be true, it would follow that he knew that God existed. Anyone who held that someone could be said without logical absurdity to know that this statement was true and yet not know that God existed would in my terminology have to deny that this statement was a theistic statement. I now append some details.

(i) The definition is not intended to imply that God does

52

exist, or that he does not, or that anyone in fact knows that he does, or knows that he does. not. (ii) It is not intended as a characterisation of all religious discourse. There are non-theistic religions, or appear to be. Manifestly, also, religious discourse contains much else in addition to statements, such as questions, requests, commands and avowals. Further, many of the statements that believers make inevitably have overtones which are absent when the same statements are made by unbelievers. The definition is merely intended to capture one feature of some crucial statements that religious discourse contains. (iii) Some decision needs to be made about the statement 'God exists' itself. Unless we specify that a statement is theistic if it could only be known to be true by someone who *also* knew that God exists, the definition as we have it would include the assertion of God's existence itself. If we exclude it, we either have to consider the apparently absurd alternative of calling it a non-theistic statement, or place it in a class by itself. Convenience suggests leaving the definition in its original form, thus making 'God exists' itself a theistic statement.

Let us now return to our earlier considerations concerning proof. We had cautiously adopted the position that God's existence cannot be proved, noting that it is still in much need of interpretation. One item of further interpretation can now be added. Let us suppose someone put together a proof of God's existence that had as one of its premisses a theistic statement. This would generate discomfort. What would the source of this discomfort be? It would not be the fact that Moore's first condition for successful proof, as we amended it, was violated, for it need not be. In making a theistic statement one need not state that God exists. The source of the 'circularity' must lie elsewhere. Clearly it comes from the fact that one could not know the premiss to be true unless one knew the conclusion to be true. In the context of many attempted proofs, such discomfort is quite legitimate. But we have refused so to define what a proof is that knowledge of the truth of the conclusion beforehand disqualifies an argument from being a successful proof, since proving can have more purposes than one. So our definition of proof allows for an argument with a theistic premiss to count. On the other hand, those who deny that there can be proofs of God's existence are likely to be impatient if offered such an argument as a counter-example. Of course our account of proof allows them to reject such an attempted proof: they can simply deny that the premiss is known to be true. But although this is so, the dispute between natural theologians and their opponents has often been about an issue which can better be characterised in another way. (It should be remembered that many of those who oppose natural theology have been theists, who might claim to know the truth of such theistic premisses, and might even on reflection not care to argue too much against proofs based on them.) The issue is often: can there be proofs of God's existence that begin with premisses that are non-theistic? Natural theology is the attempt to provide such proofs. It is certainly such proofs that critics of natural theology, whether religious sceptics or fideistic theologians, have usually had in mind when attacking the enterprise of proof. Certainly the traditional theistic proofs purport to begin from premisses that are non-theistic. Our earlier criticisms of arguments that have been supposed to show that proofs of God are impossible still apply, *a fortiori*, if we confine ourselves to proofs that begin with non-theistic premisses. I would still maintain, then, that the failure of the traditional arguments supports, but does not prove, the claim that the enterprise of trying to prove God's existence from non-theistic premisses is an impossible one.

(c) Two Versions of an Epistemological Principle

So far we have confined ourselves in our talk of religiously important proofs to proofs of the existence of God. The restriction is natural, since the familiar arguments have been of this sort. But we are now in a position to widen the scope of our discussion to include other religious statements, by formulating a principle which, if true, is of fundamental importance for the understanding of the epistemological status of religious belief. Having enunciated it, we can then proceed to refine it and assess its implications. The principle we have so far been concerned to examine is the principle that the existence of God cannot be proved; this has been narrowed to the principle that it is impossible to prove that

God exists from non-theistic premises. Having narrowed the principle in this way, let us now widen it in another. Let us widen it to cover not only proofs of God's existence, but proofs of all theistic statements. The principle then becomes: no theistic statement can be proved from a set of premises, however large, that consists exclusively of non-theistic statements.

This is a principle to which all atheists and agnostics ought to adhere, and which many theists would also accept. Its status is the same as that of the principle that no proof of God's existence is possible from non-theistic premises. Anyone committed to the latter is committed to it also. This is easy to show. For suppose someone were to succeed in proving some theistic conclusion from non-theistic premises. This means he would have proved some conclusion which can only be known to be true by someone who knows that God exists. But in any successful proof, given known premises and sound logic, the only obstacles to the hearer's knowing the conclusion to be true are irrationality or self-deception, not ignorance. So if God's existence has to be known for the conclusion to be known, it can only be because God's existence figures as one of the known premises. It could only do this in one of two ways: (a) by being added to the others, in which case the premises would no longer consist solely of non-theistic statements, or (b) by being proved from the other premises as one step in the total argument, which is also impossible if non-theistic premises cannot suffice to prove that God exists. So if the existence of God cannot be proved from non-theistic premises, neither can any other non-theistic statement be so proved. Since, therefore, these two principles have the same status, and we have already commented enough on the status of the first, nothing further needs to be said at present about the status of the second.

Let us give our principle a title. I shall here borrow and misuse a name invented in another connection by Professor Gareth Matthews (10). The doctrine that theistic statements cannot be proved from non-theistic ones I shall call 'theological non-naturalism'. It is a view to which, I would argue, all atheists and agnostics are committed, and it is also a view which many theists hold also. It is still not as precise as it needs to be, but is clearly enough stated for its importance

c

to be brought out.

I shall assume throughout that all knowledge contained in disciplines such as mathematics, physics, chemistry, biology, psychology, archaeology or history is expressible in non-theistic statements. I shall assume, in other words, that it would be intolerable to insist that any statement in any of these disciplines is of such a kind that it could only be known to be true if God's existence were also known, and I shall assume that any statement which could only be known to be true if God's existence were known could not form part of any of these disciplines. If this is true, then theistic statements cannot, by the above, be proved from premises taken from any of these disciplines. As random examples, the following would not suffice to prove any theistic conclusions:

Human beings have a deep need for love.
A vessel answering to the Biblical description of Noah's Ark has been discovered on Mount Ararat.
The suicide of Judas is vouched for by Josephus.
The solar system had a datable beginning.

It follows from our account of proof that if some statement cannot be proved from premises of a certain kind, then someone whose knowledge is confined to facts of that kind cannot be irrational in refusing to accept that statement. Hence, if theological non-naturalism is true, no one who does not know independently that God exists can be held to be irrational if he rejects a theistic interpretation of facts, such as those above, which form part of the natural or human sciences. (He may of course be *mistaken* in rejecting it.)

On the other hand, if there is someone who does know independently that God exists, and is therefore in a position to use this fact which he knows as a premiss, this person can very likely prove large numbers of theistic statements by combining this premiss with other premisses taken from these sciences. To get theistic conclusions, he only needs to have one theistic premiss: the others can be non-theistic ones. If he, or his hearers, know the truth of both the theistic and the non-theistic premisses, and the other conditions for proof are satisfied, then he and they would be irrational if they refused to accept theistic conclusions based upon them. The theist would then be in a position to acquire a large body of knowledge which the sceptic could not acquire; though he would not be in a position to accuse them of irrationality for not sharing it. Both sides would, of course, share a very large body of non-theistic knowledge. The theist's would differ from the atheist's by addition.

It is not part of my philosophical argument to urge that anyone is in fact in this position, or that no one is; for to decide this is to proceed from a prior decision that God does, or does not, exist. But there are beyond doubt many who consider themselves to be in this position. Someone who considers himself to be in this position is, I suggest, someone who has faith. We have here the beginnings of an account of what faith is.

From where the man of faith stands, he knows much that others do not know, and he can learn much more. For as his non-theistic knowledge grows, so may his theistic knowledge. There can be no legitimate connection between faith and ignorance. From where those who do not have faith stand, even though the man of faith shares with them much non-theistic knowledge, the rest that he holds is arbitrary opinion and not knowledge at all.

This is why it is so difficult to give a neutral account of the nature of faith. This difficulty has led many to try to achieve it by dropping reference to knowledge altogether in their account of it. Hick is right to resist this, for to abandon reference to knowledge is to open the door to obscurantism and make those who have faith feel a quite inappropriate discomfort about the indefinite enlargement of the secular facts which their faith can be thought to illuminate. If a neutral account of faith is possible at all, however, it should be in terms of the possession of knowledge, or the conviction of its possession. The disjunction has to be used. Of course someone who thinks he has knowledge is not committed by this to holding that his knowledge cannot be enlarged, or his understanding of what he knows deepened. He can enlarge it now by basing further proofs on it. He can expect his understanding of what he thinks he knows to be deepened at some later time, or verified. Of this, more later.

The principle of theological non-naturalism, then, is of

considerable importance for understanding what faith is and what separates the man who has faith from the man who does not. Since it is so important, it is necessary to ensure it is free of ambiguities. As it has been stated so far it contains one major ambiguity which has to be removed before any further implications can be explored. As so far stated, it says merely that it is not possible to prove any theistic statement from premises which are wholly non-theistic. But there are several conditions for successful proof; so there are several possible reasons why an attempted proof may fail. Someone who claims that all attempted proofs of theistic conclusions that begin with non-theistic premises must fail has not, thus far, indicated which of the possible reasons will lead to the failure. He may not have thought about this detail very clearly, but it is important to consider it.

I shall assume that in any attempted proof of a theistic conclusion from non-theistic premises the first Moorean condition, as amended, is satisfied: that the conclusion is a statement that has not already been made in the statement of the premises. This still allows that such an argument may fail because not all the premises are true; or because not all are known to be true; or because even if true and known to be, they do not entail the conclusion or render it overwhelmingly probable. Now although it is a very big claim to say that all arguments of a certain sort must always fall foul of one or other of these standards, the fact that all these standards are involved in proof allows someone who does not accept the conclusion of an attempted proof a considerable range of rational choice when he tries to fasten upon his grounds for rejecting it. It enables him to choose whether to reject it on the grounds that the premises are not true, or not known to be, or on the ground that even if they were true, and known to be true, they still would not suffice to establish the conclusion. It is this latter ambiguity that is critical for us. As so far defined, theological non-naturalism allows anyone to say that there are certain non-theistic statements which would, in his view, be sufficient to prove some theistic conclusion, but which happen, as a matter of fact, not to be true, or not to be known to be true. Many of those who have rejected particular theistic proofs seem to have taken this position. At least some of the time in Hume's 'Dialogues

Concerning Natural Religion' (during the discussion of evil, for example) it seems to be implied that although the world as we find it does not contain the features which would serve to show, with the conclusiveness that Cleanthes proclaims, that the world was designed by a benevolent divine intelligence, this might be shown conclusively if only the world were different, e.g. free of suffering. This is a common enough position, and one, again, which many believers also take, recognising (and indeed emphasising) that a world that needs God may not be one the examination of which proves that he is there.

Let us now imagine ourselves undertaking an inquisitorial exercise. Let us imagine ourselves asking some particular theological non-naturalist a series of questions designed to elicit from him which non-theistic statements he would regard as sufficient to prove a theistic conclusion, if only he knew them to be true. Would he think that the occurrence of a certain number of medically inexplicable recoveries at Lourdes would show that God cared for the sick? Would he think that the fact that certain mediums had conversed with departed spirits who had told them that God had preserved them from death would show that God does preserve men from death? Suppose, more radically perhaps, that all persons who let atheistic sentiments escape their lips were stricken dumb? Suppose that every Sunday night the stars in the sky over London formed themselves for three hours into the letters of the sentence PRAISE THE LORD? Suppose it were the case that every innocent sufferer of whom he had knowledge had his or her character greatly improved by suffering? Or suppose someone managed to demonstrate from impeccable metaphysical premises that this is the best of all possible worlds (11)? As these questions, however fanciful, proceeded, one might very well expect disagreement among respondents over the probative value of this or that imagined fact, and one might also expect individuals to hesitate in their interpretation of one or another of them. But sooner or later one might expect a parting of the ways among those we have so far classed as theological non-naturalists. Sooner or later it would appear that some of them would be prepared to agree that there are some non-theistic statements which, if only they were true, would be sufficient to prove that some theistic statement is true; these I shall call 'moderate' theological non-naturalists. For others, however, there are in fact *no* non-theistic statements which, even if true, would be allowed by them to prove any theistic conclusion; these I shall call 'radical' theological non-naturalists. For the radical theological non-naturalist, no non-theistic statement whatever, however much it reported a world different from the one we in fact live in, would be allowed to show conclusively that any theistic claim is true. Someone, on the other hand, who adopts moderate theological non-naturalism and holds that even though theistic statements cannot be proved from non-theistic ones, this is merely because the premises that would prove them are not premises that anyone will ever know to be true ones, is admitting that it is possible to envisage situations which could in principle be known to obtain by someone who did not know that God exists, and yet could serve, if they only did obtain, to prove to that person some truth about God.

Although individual theological non-naturalists may not have chosen between these two views, it is important to see that both are possible. The purpose of much traditional natural theology was to show that in the face of certain facts which could be ascertained by someone who did not know that God exists, it is irrational to deny that he does exist. The theological non-naturalist is someone who denies that there are actually facts accessible to such a person of which this is true. The radical version of theological non-naturalism insists that there could be none; that nothing could make it irrational to refuse to accept any theistic conclusion if one does not have some knowledge of God already. Of course, the moderate theological non-naturalist, who thinks that there could be some facts in principle which would make it irrational to reject a theistic conclusion, but are not, does not necessarily mean by this that these facts would entail the theistic conclusion: only that any other logically possible explanation of those facts would be an irrational one to prefer. Someone who wavers over a particular example is presumably trying to decide whether or not it would be irrational to prefer some stretched non-theistic explanation of those imagined facts to the theistic one that it is alleged would be proved by them. This raises a natural question.

60

How is one to decide whether the theistic choice is or is not the only rational one in such circumstances? Is one left with the shocking subjectivity of what it seems reasonable or unreasonable to accept as sufficient to establish some conclusion? Are we faced with the ultimate philosopher's horror of having to use our judgement? Or are there general criteria that we can use to determine such a decision?

There are two general considerations which would decide the matter, but which I suggest should be put aside. One simple way to justify radical theological non-naturalism would be to prove that God could not exist. This one could do by showing that the concept of God contains contradictions. If one could do this, one could justify a negative evaluation of any and every suggested probative premiss. I have had to assume without demonstration that this move is not available. I will merely point out that it is not, of course, a move that all atheists are committed to; for the atheist, though committed to the moderate form of theological non-naturalism, can reject its radical form, since he can hold that there are propositions which, were they only true, would show that God existed; they might be the contradictories of propositions which he does think are true and show in his view that God does not. Another general sort of consideration that could be brought in in some instances is that the concept of God has built into it certain attributes which show that if God existed the fact imagined in the alleged probative proposition would never be the case. It might be said, for example, that a world in which outspoken atheists were struck dumb would not show on pain of irrationality that God existed because even though we might be frightened in such a world into accepting that God existed, the concept of God is the concept of a being free of malevolent bursts of temper; so if we succumbed to these phenomena we would be calling some other less admirable being by too complimentary a title. Objections of this sort might very well defeat particular imagined inferences; but they would not undermine more than a modest number. For unless one were to adopt the quite indefensible position that the world we have is the only one which God, if he exists, could have created, it will never be impossible to think up descriptions of better worlds in which it might be less

61

obviously rational to deny his existence than it is in this one.

Another general consideration that suggests itself is that the conclusion that some theistic statement is true is a very important sort of conclusion to draw, and therefore one on which it is proper to withhold one's judgement for as long as one conceivably can. This looks like a counsel of prudence in favour of refraining from jumping to theistic conclusions, and might seem to weigh against the intrinsic stringency of any imagined inference. But it is not so very clear which way prudential considerations ought to sway us in these matters. We can brush aside the suggestion that prudential considerations are enough to tell us which way to draw our conclusions. But if, *ex hypothesi,* there is some need to look for others, there seems no good reason to exclude prudential ones. But if one admits them at all, then they seem to be distinctly double-edged. Against the claim that theistic beliefs have such far-reaching practical implications that they ought not to be adopted unless the evidence is compelling is the simple counter-argument, which all readers of Pascal (12) know, that these beliefs have such far-reaching practical implications that one had better *not fail* to adopt them unless there are cogent reasons for not doing so. The importance of religious claims should certainly make us look at them hard. But looking at them hard is not the same as looking at them sceptically.

A more plausible general consideration is that of economy and complexity. It seems obvious that some account of an apparently probative fact that does not involve reference to divine agency or divine wishes is a more economical account than the one that would be implied if the fact were allowed to prove divine agency or divine wishes. It may *seem* obvious, but it becomes less so on reflection. Against the apparent economy of non-theistic accounts of some imagined facts one has, first, to weigh their intrinsic implausibility in the very striking cases, and the coincidences and anomalies that give rise to it. The sorts of cases that would offer themselves as likely candidates for probative status would require a good many explanatory epicycles, as it were, to account for them naturalistically. One has, then, to weigh the economy of the naturalistic account (in the sense of its relative parsimony with entities) against its theoretical complexity. But in addition to this one has to weigh it against the vague but recognisable claims of explanatory depth. The man who accepts that certain facts would prove God's existence or agency need not deny that naturalistic accounts of them can be given, but he will deny that they escape a fatal superficiality. And he will argue that the appropriateness of a standard in one field does not guarantee its force in another. These considerations are very vague and general, but I think recognisable. In order to decide between them one must confront, one by one, test cases that involve them, and give up hope of settling them at a higher level of generality. For it is hard to see what general epistemological considerations can be brought to bear upon them, except those that depend on a decision about the truth or falsity of the very theistic claims the imagined facts are supposed to prove or fail to prove.

We do seem, then, to be unable to escape very easily from individual judgement that this or that inference from some imagined non-theistic fact to some theistic conclusion would constitute a proof of it, or would not; that it would or would not render that conclusion overwhelmingly likely, or show it to be true conclusively, or put it beyond reasonable doubt. None of these is an evaluative expression that it is easy, or even perhaps possible, to define very exactly - as one can see if one reflects for a moment on how hard it would be to define the notion of overwhelming likelihood in terms of frequency. Yet if he cannot demonstrate logical contradictions in the concept of God, a radical theological non-naturalist is also forced back upon justifying his stance by reference to a series of individual judgements that this, that, or the other premiss would fail to prove a theistic conclusion. Yet this would supply him with no grounds for his negative position, since he would never, presumably, be prepared to say what premises would be free of the inadequacies that he claimed to detect in the ones he rejected. And without such preparedness his position is wholly arbitrary. The situation, therefore, appears to be that when presented with a series of allegedly probative imaginary premisses, and asked whether they would or would not put theistic conclusions beyond reasonable doubt, we do not have any non-question-begging general principles to appeal to in reaching our decisions; yet it is still irrational to insist that no imaginary premiss whatsoever could have the required probative force. We may bewail, if we wish, having to depend on individual judgement without the aid of general principles, though life is very often like that; but we should bewail much more loudly any *a priori* insistence that this judgement must always be exercised in one direction. There is no good reason to think that we could not, with a little ingenuity, think up some non-theistic statements which would serve, if true, to put some theistic conclusions beyond reasonable doubt. So theistic statements are not immune to indirect proof in principle, even if the outlook for proving them in practice is completely gloomy. The facts as we know them may not be sufficient to prove them, but it is irrational to insist that nothing could.

If this is true, let us now look at the disagreement between the believer and the sceptic. Both can agree that a certain indirect proof of God's existence, or of some theistic statement, would be a sound one. Both may further agree that although it would be a sound one the premisses of it are not true, or not known to be true, to anyone who does not already know that God exists. The sceptic, who does not have knowledge that God exists, will now justify his scepticism by pointing out that inductive considerations make it very unlikely that such premisses will ever be true, or will ever be known to be true. The world as it is is not such as to provide us with such a proof, as Hume showed us so convincingly in the 'Dialogues', and ordinary inductive considerations make it very unlikely indeed that it will change radically enough to do so, as Hume reminded us in his essay on 'Miracles' (13). The believer, on the other hand, thinks he knows that God exists. He may still not think it any more likely than the sceptic does that the world will provide the material for a sound indirect proof of this fact. But whatever position he may take about the likelihood of some probative events coming to pass, the fact that he considers himself to know that God exists enables him, if he wishes, to prove to his own satisfaction all sorts of other theistic conclusions - if he combines non-theistic premisses, which the unbeliever could also accept, with theistic ones which he can claim to know independently. The proofs that may result from this will naturally be rejected by the sceptic, since they will depend on premisses some of which he will deny to be true; but if the believer really does know their truth, and his arguments have all the other prerequisites of good proofs, they will be good proofs in spite of the sceptic's objections. They will just not convince him. Such in-group exercises are by no means pointless; I take it that arguments like this are not uncommon in theological disputes between theists. For example if one theist wishes to prove to another that p, he may be able to show that some scriptural text states or implies that p. This is something that the sceptic could agree to. He can then combine with this minor premiss some major premiss to the effect that the text in question has divine authority. These two together will prove that p, for anyone who knows both the major and the minor to be true. The sceptic will reject it because he will deny that the major is true, or at least that it is known to be. But if the theist constructing the proof and the theist for whom he constructs it do know that the major is true, then they have a sound proof of p and the sceptic is wrong. Of course all this requires knowledge that propositions like this major premiss are true.

I have spoken so far only about proving propositions about God. It is obvious enough that even though they may expect certain probative statements to turn out in the long run to be true, many Christian theists do not look for this. So I will turn for the present to a closely allied question, that of the possibility of verifying theistic statements. This notion has been discussed a good deal recently in the philosophy of religion because of the writings of John Hick, and of those sceptical critics he has tried to answer.

4 Faith and Verification

(a) The Verificationist Legacy

There is a tendency today to think of discussions of the concept of verification as out of date, and to feel that philosophers of religion who concern themselves with its place in religious thought merely show how far they are behind their colleagues. This is a pity, for although much of the talk of the verifiability of religious claims is indeed out of date, the consideration of this issue has stimulated one of the most valuable additions to our understanding of the nature of faith in recent years. I refer here to Hick's discussion of eschatological verification(1). This chapter consists of comments on what Hick has said, and of applications of his lessons to the matters raised earlier.

The reason that the reaction of many philosophers to talk of verification is one of impatience is that most discussion of this notion has in fact been about the Verification Principle(2). This principle was designed to serve as a criterion for separating meaningful statements from meaningless ones, by stipulating that the former were in principle verifiable by sense-experience and the latter not. This enterprise was historically (and contingently) connected with a programme of phenomenalistic analysis of common-sense and scientific statements, the purpose of which was to show that the content of such statements can be reduced ultimately to that of reports, or groups of reports, of sense-experiences. At one point during the long course of the discussion of the feasibility of this programme and the utility of the principle, Ayer drew a famous distinction between a strong and a weak version of the principle: the strong version being said to be the claim that for a statement to be meaningful it had to be conclusively verifiable by sense-experience, the weak version being the claim that for a statement to be meaningful it was merely necessary for sense-experience to be relevant to its truth(3). With a rare deference to common usage, the proponents of the principle did not go on to distinguish between conclusive and inconclusive verification; instead of this, one had talk of sense-experiences confirming meaningful statements, or making them probable.

The major reason why conclusive verification was abandoned as a criterion of meaning was that an enormous number of statements that were clearly meaningful and were also admitted by verificationists to be so, were excluded by the strong version of the principle. The cases most commonly referred to are general statements, such as 'All crows are black', or material-object statements, such as 'This book is red'. A general statement could always be denied without contradiction by someone who admitted the existence of any finite number of supporting instances: however many crows he had seen that were black, he could still deny that all crows are black without thereby contradicting all the statements he had agreed to previously about the blackness of individual observed crows. Material-object statements, it seemed, could always be denied without contradiction by someone who had admitted to the truth of any finite number of statements of how it looked to him, or to other observers, that the book was red. Since no contradiction would occur in either of these cases, it was felt, it could not be the case that the general statement or the material-object statement were equivalent in meaning to the statements of sense-experience that supported them. In a context where a stated philosophical objective was the establishment of the truth of phenomenalism, this was often thought to justify the view that general statements and material-object statements were not conclusively verifiable, and could only be confirmed or rendered probable by observations. The truth behind this rather curious reasoning is the undoubted fact that indeed no finite accumulation of observation-statements entails either of the statements referred to; so they cannot be equivalent in meaning to them either. As long as the verifiability of a statement was being used in the context of a possible reductive analysis, it was only too easy to assume that this sound point of logic was sufficient to show that the statements under examination were not conclusively

67

verifiable.

But this conclusion depends on the assumption that no statement can be conclusively verified unless the statements reporting the observations that support it jointly entail it. Outside the context of an attempt at reductive analysis, such an assumption appears quite groundless(4). The accumulation of facts of a certain kind may serve to verify a statement even though they do not entail it. For they may, as Hick says, put it beyond reasonable doubt. In so far as there is a common use of the concept of verification, as distinct from semi-technical uses it may be given at times in philosophical literature, the core of it seems to be what Hick says that it is(5). What follows is intended to be a partial account of a real and common use of the notion. As in the case of our discussion of proof, one operates here in an area where clear definitions do not lie ready to hand and where more than one sense no doubt exists; but it would be a fatal flaw in the account if it were to turn out to be merely stipulative.

(It is worth while to mention here that once the notion of conclusive verification is separated from that of entailment, it is possible to present the verification principle in a form that still refers to conclusive verification without being thereby committed to the possibility of a phenomenalistic translation of all meaningful statements. One might claim - though I would not - that all meaningful statements are statements with regard to which it is possible to state what observations would conclusively verify them, even though such statements would not entail them, or mean the same as they mean. One is not forced to settle for the mere relevance of sense-experience, with its notorious permissiveness, because phenomenalism collapses.)

(b) The Nature of Verification

Let us begin with the account of the concept of verification which John Hick offers in Chapter 8 of 'Faith and Knowledge'. Briefly summarised, it runs as follows. Verification should be construed (as we recommended that proof should be construed) as a performance that someone goes through, rather than as a relation between propositions. To verify a proposition is to show that there is no room for rational doubt as to its truth. Verification, thus understood, does not take place unless someone knows that it has: the facts that verify the proposition must be known to someone who can see that they remove any grounds for rational doubt of the proposition that they verify. The procedure that will lead to the knowledge of the verificatory facts is one that can be described in conditional predictions. Even though someone must be aware of a proposition's being verified for it to be verified, this awareness could be restricted to certain individuals or groups, and might not be available universally. Finally, Hick stresses, as we have above, the difference between verification and 'logical certification', though he refers to 'logical certification or proof'. This is not an account with which I have any fundamental disagreement, but it does require amplification, and some emendation.

There seems to be a distinction between direct and indirect verification that parallels our earlier distinction between direct and indirect proof. A shopkeeper may say that his calculations indicate there is (he will probably say 'there must be' or 'there should be') £23.25 in the till; he may then ask his assistant to verify this by counting what is there. In such a case a claim or a tentative conclusion is verified by someone's independently ascertaining the truth of that which is claimed or tentatively concluded. This sort of case would seem to qualify naturally for the title of direct verification. On the other hand, there seem to be many cases where one verifies some claim or assertion that p, by ascertaining the truth of some other assertion that q, which is sufficient to establish it. I may verify the claim of my Member of Parliament that he spoke in favour of a certain bill in the House of Commons by reading 'Hansard'; a doctor can verify the detective's theory that the victim was dead before midnight by ascertaining the condition of the corpse. In these cases what one ascertains in the course of verifying that p is not *that p*, but *that q* (that 'Hansard' quotes the Member as uttering certain sentences, that the corpse is in such-and-such a condition), where the fact that q puts the statement that p beyond reasonable doubt. No doubt there are borderline cases: if I ascertain that my uncle says in his will that Jones is to be his heir, do I verify Jones's statement that he is my uncle's heir directly or indirectly? But borderline cases do not destroy a real distinction. I shall be concerned throughout with the concept of indirect verification.

Let us accept the preference for considering verification as a procedure or activity, rather than as a relationship between propositions, as we did in the case of proof. The temptation to do otherwise would probably be less strong in this case, but we do not need to argue it is absurd in order to have a rational preference for our own procedure. It is not my purpose in what follows to claim precise parallels between proving and verifying; but the similarities are of more importance for us than the differences. One difference is that verifying that p may involve the procedure of ascertaining that q, whereas even if one proves p using q as a premiss it would be unnatural to speak of the ascertaining of the truth of q as itself part of the process of proving that p. But this difference is not crucial in the cases that will most concern us.

We need not linger on the need for the statement used to verify some conclusion being different from the statement it is used to verify. As in the case of proof, this condition can be interpreted to mean that it must not be necessary to state the latter in order to state the former. The need for this condition is based ultimately on the fact that it is indirect proof and indirect verification that we have to characterise. The second condition of proof, that the probative statement must be a true one, also applies: it would be paradoxical to state that one can use a false statement to verify any conclusion. The important questions come up when we consider the verificatory counterparts to the third and fourth conditions of proof. Since the fourth can be dealt with fairly briefly, I will take it first. Hick is clearly right to insist that what verifies some proposition does not need to be something from which that proposition follows. Indeed, not only does this emerge as the conclusion of our earlier comments on verification; in this case, as opposed to that of proof, instances where the relationship is one of entailment would be much rarer than instances where the relationship is the one we would express by saying that the evidence rendered the conclusion overwhelmingly likely, or put it beyond reasonable doubt, but did not entail it. It does not follow, however, as Hick appears to think, that the conclusion *cannot* be a logical consequence of the verificatory statements: would the assistant's ascertaining that there were £19 in the till not verify the shopkeeper's statement that there was less than £20 there? Hick seems doubly mistaken in distinguishing verification from 'logical certification or proof': he is wrong in equating these two, since not all proof involves entailment; and he is wrong in implying that verification can never do so(6).

It is the third condition, relating to knowledge of the verificatory statements and the conclusions they support, that gives asymmetries between the person-relativity of proof and of verification. Can a statement be verified if it is already known to be true? The inclination to respond negatively to this question is somewhat greater than the inclination to respond negatively to the parallel question about proof. It seems most natural to say that what is verified has to be some statement towards which some degree of doubt still exists, or is at least still reasonable, so that even if a person to or for whom the statement is verified is already convinced of its truth, his state of mind with regard to it falls short of knowledge prior to the verification. On the other hand, a parallel with the case of proving something for someone who already knows it seems to exist when we reflect that it seems quite natural to speak of investigators producing new verifications for some theory that is already regarded as established, thus reinforcing our understanding of its truth and its ramifications; perhaps they might be said to have verified it for us (though certainly not to us), although this form of words seems still to suggest that we were uncertain of the truth of that which they have verified. I shall suggest below a way of accommodating these competing inclinations without resorting to two senses of 'verify', but it seems clear that the parallel with proof is not exact here.

Let us investigate this further by distinguishing between a person who claims that some statement is true, a person who performs the process of verification, and a person for whom the verifying is done. They may be identical with each other, or they may not. To talk always in the passive about p's being verified is to obscure the differences between these three roles; and even if we use the active voice and talk only of verifying that p, there is still a risk of overlooking the distinction between the second and the third. Let us call someone who makes the claim that p the 'claimant', one who does the verifying the 'investigator', and one to or for whom p is verified the 'hearer'. This enables us to clarify the relationship between verification and previous knowledge.

There seems no reason why the claimant cannot know that p already, though of course he may not. Nor is there any reason why the investigator should not know that p already. The preceding does suggest, however, that it is at least most untypical for the hearer to be someone who knows that p already. If this is sound, then it suggests that if a claimant knows that p already, the claimant and hearer will not be identical, or that if the investigator knows that p already, then the investigator and the hearer will not be identical; but if either of them does not know that p already, then he can be identical with the hearer. The word 'claimant' is perhaps misleading, but is not here intended to imply conviction, merely some degree of positive epistemic inclination. Someone who is inclined to some statement can get someone else, who may, unlike himself, know it to be true (or may not), to verify it for him (or for others).

Of course a statement can be verified in response not to a claim that it is true, but to a denial of its truth. But then the denier, if he need figure in our scheme at all, would have to figure as the hearer, and the claimant will be someone against whom the denial has been made; in these circumstances the investigator could be either party, or neither, but could not be both.

These last reflections raise the question how far it is essential to have anyone in any of these roles. It seems quite in order to say that someone could prove a statement to be true without setting out to do so, viz. by finding the statement to be that to which the knowledge he already has inevitably points; it is even possible to set out to prove one thing and end up having proved another, which no one at all has offered as the truth previously. But it seems odd to speak of verifying some proposition which has not been offered by some claimant as at least a reasonably likely truth. So some claimant appears to be necessary for verification to take place. On the other hand, no investigator seems necessary, once we cease to concentrate on the case of experimental verification, where an investigator goes through a deliberate procedure in order to establish the verificatory information. Just as something can be proved by events, so even more clearly can it be verified by events. Perhaps it is true that for a claim to be verified someone must verify it, but this does not mean that there has to be someone who, as investigator, is causally responsible for generating the verificatory phenomena, or does research and assembles information; at most it means that there must be a hearer who recognises facts which put the statement verified beyond reasonable doubt, and such facts can force themselves on the hearer's attention. Most difficult of all, must there always be a hearer? The problem here is not the case where the claimant and hearer are one and the same, and there has been a process of placing beyond reasonable doubt some statement that he was at first merely inclined to believe. The problem is the case where the claimant could not be a hearer because the claimant already knows that p; and then events transpire, or information becomes available, to put p beyond reasonable doubt for anyone who did not previously know it; in such a case would it be improper to say that p had been verified by these events or by this information, even if, by ill-fortune, no one but the claimant himself was aware of this? It seems mistaken to deny that p has been verified, but also mistaken to say that it has been verified to, or even for, the claimant, since he already knew it. His knowledge has perhaps been reinforced, his claim to knowledge perhaps confirmed or vindicated; and all this would show hearers, were there any, how right he had been. But p has not, it seems, been verified for him. The only way out seems to be to stay obstinately with the passive and say that p has been verified, and the claimant can see it has been verified, but no one has verified it, and it has not been verified to or for anyone. These types of case may be rare, but seem intelligible enough, and perhaps they show that there need be no hearer to or for whom p is verified, for p to be verified. Even if p cannot be verified unless someone knows that it has, this condition may be satisfied not only when there is a hearer for whom p is verified, but also when there is a claimant who, though knowing p to be true before, now sees that it is verified, even though to or for no one. In either situation, the person who fulfils this condition for verification must know what p is, must know the facts that place it beyond reasonable doubt, and be able to see that this is how they stand in relation to p.

Suppose there is a hearer, and that he satisfies all these conditions. Does he then have to know that p? It seems here that the situation is parallel to that of proof. Just as a person to whom p has been proved may still not clearly know that p, because of irrationality or self-deception, so it may happen that someone to whom p has been verified may still not clearly know that p, for the same reasons. He may only know very well that p. Conversely, someone who, in these circumstances, does not clearly know that p because of irrationality or self-deception, still can have had p verified to him, whatever he may say about the matter.

Hick seems to be right when he says that there is nothing in the concept of verification to require that everyone is qualified to function in any of the verificatory roles we have distinguished. It may require expert knowledge to make a claim, or perform an investigation, or be in a position to recognise that the key facts are to hand and have the import that they do. It may require a doctor to verify the claims of a detective. We must postpone the consideration of Hick's further argument that the verification of theistic claims might be confined to the faithful.

With these detailed emendations we can now proceed, on the basis of Hick's account of what verification is. We are now in a position to connect our understanding of verification with the results of our previous discussions. Although there are asymmetries between indirect verification and indirect proof, these are asymmetries about the activities and previous knowledge of those involved in proving or verifying. The epistemic weight and function of the premiss in a successful proof and the verificatory statement in a successful verification are the same. From this we can infer that if some statement were sufficient to prove some other statement, p, to be true, then in appropriate contexts of claimant and investigator and hearer, it might equally well serve to verify that p; and conversely. I do not wish to assert that every statement which would serve to prove some other would also serve to verify that other; but if our account of the two concepts and their likenesses is correct, it would seem to follow that this would be true as a rule. If this is so, then two other conclusions can be drawn.

1. A theological non-naturalist must hold that no theistic statement can be verified by reference to any set of non-theistic statements, however large. He must hold, that is, that if any non-theistic statement is offered in purported verification of some theistic claim, it is either not itself known to be true, or is such that even if it were known to be true, it would not suffice to place the theistic claim beyond reasonable doubt.

2. A radical theological non-naturalist must hold that no set of non-theistic statements, however large, can, even if known to be true, be sufficient to verify any theistic statement. This might be put by saying that for the radical theological non-naturalist theistic statements are in principle unverifiable by non-theistic statements.

All atheists and agnostics are committed to theological non-naturalism as expressed in 1. This can readily be proved, if it is accepted that the atheist and agnostic are committed to at least moderate theological non-naturalism about proof of theistic statements. If one holds to this, one must hold to the corresponding view of verification of theistic statements. Suppose that someone has had verified to him some theistic statement by ascertaining the truth of non-theistic statements only. The statement he has then had verified to him is one the truth of which he can only know if he knows that God exists. But if the verification has been successful, all that can stand in the way of his knowledge, given his knowledge of these non-theistic statements, is irrationality or self-deception, not ignorance of God's existence. So if the theistic statement cannot be known unless God's existence is known, either God's existence has been assumed as part of the verification procedure, or it has been proved from the non-theistic statements ascertained to be true during that procedure. The latter is excluded by our assumption that non-theistic premises are insufficient to prove the existence of God. So the theistic statement has only been verified by assuming the existence of God in addition to ascertaining the truth of the verificatory non-theistic statements. So the verification cannot have taken place solely by reference to non-theistic statements. So no one who holds to theological non-naturalism about proof is entitled to admit the possibility of theistic statements being verified by reference solely to non-theistic ones.

This does not, however, do anything to establish the truth of radical theological non-naturalism. Indeed, I would argue that here, as in the parallel case of proof, radical theological non-naturalism is an arbitrary and absurd thesis, incapable of being justified except by resort to arguments that beg critical questions about the truth or falsity of theistic statements themselves.

None of the above shows that one theistic statement cannot be verified by ascertaining the truth of another theistic statement. Nor does it show that someone who already knows that God exists could not verify a theistic statement by ascertaining the truth of non-theistic ones and combining this with the explicit or implicit appeal to his knowledge of God's existence. For someone who knew that God existed, therefore, it might well be that both theistic and non-theistic facts could serve to verify claims that he might make or hear about God's nature or dealings with men. All this is quite consistent with the truth of theological non-naturalism; and it might occur frequently. All that is inconsistent with theological non-naturalism is that verification of theistic statements should be possible for someone whose knowledge is confined to non-theistic facts. Such a person could not participate in the in-group exercises in verification which the man who knew of God's existence could engage in; but these exercises could be, and are, of great importance in the daily lives of those who consider themselves to have this knowledge.

A person who considers himself in this position of having access to verification of his and others' claims about God is, I submit, someone who has faith. This is a partial indication of what faith is, couched in the language of knowledge. Those who lack faith must of course regard the non-theistic facts the man of faith presses into service in this way as being misused to consolidate a set of illusions.

(c) Verification and Religious Discourse

Some critics of religious discourse in our day have said that it lacks meaning because it is unverifiable. In order to preserve the elementary distinction between meaninglessness and falsity, this has to be read as 'unverifiable in principle'. The criticism is not that as a matter of fact no one is in a position to verify religious claims, but that it is not possible to say what would verify them. The exact implications of this for those elements of religious discourse other than theistic statements need not concern us. How radical this criticism of religious statements is depends on whether it is held that religious claims are unverifiable by reference to theistic or non-theistic statements. If the criticism is a wholly general one to the effect that there is no place for the notion of verification within religious discourse at all, it is quite in order to counter this by pointing out that theistic statements can serve to verify one another: for example, that claims about God's attitudes to men can be verified by reference to God's behaviour towards the Jews in Old Testament times. The intent in most cases, however, appears to be to make a claim which this would not answer: the claim appears to be that theistic statements ought to be, but are not, verifiable by reference to non-theistic statements alone. We must be clear what this view is. It is not, once again, the view that as a matter of fact there are no verificatory non-theistic facts for theistic statements, for this is a view about our ability to know the truth about theistic statements; what we now have before us is a view about their meaning. It must therefore be the view that they do not have meaning because it is not possible for us to say what non-theistic statements, if known to be true, would serve to verify them. This view entails radical theological non-naturalism. I have argued that this is an arbitrary view and ought to be rejected. But the view before us, though objectionable on this ground, is not identical with radical theological non-naturalism; it is even more extreme. For the thesis before us now is this: that only if it were possible to specify what non-theistic statements would verify theistic statements can the latter be admitted to be meaningful; and in fact it is not possible to specify this, hence they are not meaningful. It is not enough here merely to stress the irrationality of radical theological non-naturalism, for this is merely to contest the minor premiss of this argument. We must also look at the major premiss.

Let us call the combined thesis that theistic statements would, if meaningful, be verifiable in principle by reference to non-theistic ones, but that they are not, 'theological positivism'. This states a certain criterion of meaning, and also states that theistic statements fail to satisfy it. I see no good reason why religious discourse should have to meet the standard of meaningfulness that this position foists upon it. On the other hand, even though there is no reason why it should have to, our earlier discussions suggest that it does. Some misguided thinkers, trying to show that it can meet it merely because they felt the obligation to assume that it ought to do so, have tried to reduce theistic statements to non-theistic ones. An acceptance of the standard implied in theological positivism has been one of the many motives behind the attempted de-supernaturalisation of Christianity. We might dub the thesis that in the end there are no irreducibly theistic statements, 'theological phenomenalism'. It can take the form of attempting to translate theistic statements into statements about human nature and its needs, or into statements about the adoption of secular moral policies; we find such moves in the work of the 'Death of God' theologians, or in R. B. Braithwaite(7). It can also take the form of attempting to replace theology by a secular ontology, as in many parts of the writings of Paul Tillich(8). It is not necessary, or even now common, for theological positivists or theological phenomenalists to hold that the statements which verify theistic ones, or into which they are translatable, must be reports of sense-experience; though one does occasionally find an unconscious parody of this view in those who suggest that theistic statements can be reduced to statements reporting the religious experiences of those who utter them(9). Theological phenomenalism is not refutable, since its obvious critical difficulty, that it eliminates the very elements in religious discourse that it is allegedly defending, is embraced by its adherents as its greatest strength. So I will resist the temptation to show how it achieves this self-styled victory. It is sufficient here to point out that the theological non-naturalist must reject theological phenomenalism, since the latter denies the very distinction on which theological non-naturalism rests.

The radical theological non-naturalist may accept theological positivism, though he does not have to do so (for he could hold that theistic statements are in principle unverifiable but not for that reason devoid of meaning). The moderate theological non-naturalist must reject theological positivism because he holds that it is possible to say what non-theistic statements would verify theistic ones; but he has an open option whether to adopt the major premiss of theological positivism or to reject it, since he is not committed either to holding or to denying the claim that the meaning-standard of the theological positivist ought to be met, merely by admitting that it is met.

Theological positivism received its most influential expression in the 'Theology and Falsification' controversy, initiated by Antony Flew(10). The most interesting attempt to answer it has been Hick's doctrine of eschatological verification(11). This seems to amount to the thesis that the demands of theological positivism can be met by Christian religious discourse, though I am not in all respects certain of the correctness of this interpretation.

Flew's critique of theism amounts to the following. Theists and atheists appear on the surface to have different expectations of what will happen in the world, in consequence of their different beliefs about God. The one believes that God loves his creatures, and the other does not believe this. When pressed, however, the believer will not admit that any actual or imagined calamities could show his beliefs about God's love to be false, so the appearance of differing expectations is a deceptive one. This shows that the terms the theist uses to speak of God (like the word 'loves') are being covertly emptied of their normal content, since in the secular contexts from which religious discourse borrows them, any statement in which they are used is verifiable or falsifiable by reference to future events or actions. Hence theistic assertions are not genuine assertions but only look like genuine assertions. This critique appears to entail the doctrine I have called theological positivism.

Hick's response, briefly summarised, is as follows. Although the theist and the atheist will interpret day-to-day happenings in different ways, they do not, or need not, differ over what happenings to expect. This is true, however, only with regard to their expectations about this life. The believer, however, expects there to be an after-life, which the unbeliever does not anticipate. The believer further expects that in the after-life the ambiguities of this world will be removed and his claims about the love of God will be verified. If it is necessary to show that Christian claims are verifiable in order to show that they are meaningful, these eschatological predictions suffice for the purpose: if they are false, then the Christian claims will thereby be falsified.

Let us assume that there are no insuperable logical difficulties about the concept of post-mortem existence(12). There is still an important difficulty of interpretation to contend with. Is Hick claiming that Christianity can meet the demands of theological positivism? Is he, that is to say, maintaining that the post-mortem state which would verify the claim that God loves us is one that can be described in wholly non-theistic statements, or, at least, that enough of the predicted state can be described non-theistically to provide the required verification? If his intent is merely to demonstrate that Christian doctrines have a verification structure built into them, it is not necessary to add to this any further claim that the verificatory future experiences include any that could be recognised by someone who did not know that God existed. For it would still be true that the believer expected certain states and experiences to come to pass which the sceptic did not expect, and the verification or falsification would be the result of these states and experiences coming to pass or failing to do so. I incline, however, to think that Hick intends, as far as possible, to show that Christianity meets the criterion of meaningfulness presupposed in Flew's contribution to the Theology and Falsification debate, which in our terms is the criterion of theological positivism: that the statements included within Christian religious discourse can be accepted as meaningful only if it can be shown that they are in principle verifiable by circumstances which could be described in wholly non-theistic statements. To show that Christian discourse satisfies this criterion it is not of course necessary to deny that there are also expectations that must be expressed in theistic assertions; it is merely necessary to show that there are some predictions that are an integral part of that discourse, are expressible in non-theistic assertions, and would, if true, provide verification of the central doctrinal pronouncements of the faith. I think Hick is successful in showing that there are such predictions. (If it is mistaken to read him as attempting to show this, then what follows can be taken as an attempt to indicate how such a task could be accomplished using the arguments that he provides for another purpose.)

Let us begin by noting that it is quite consistent to accept Hick's doctrine of eschatological verification, as interpreted, and also to accept theological non-naturalism in its moderate form. For in the face of a particular set of predictions about the after-life, a theological non-naturalist could react in at least three ways. He could agree that if the predicted states of affairs came to pass, they would indeed verify some of the critical theistic statements which express central Christian doctrines, but could go on to say that in his view these predictions will never turn out to be true, or will never be known to have done so. He could, alternatively, hold that even if they did turn out to be true and to be known to have done so, they would not suffice to verify the theistic statements which it is alleged they would verify, even though other post-mortem states of affairs would serve to do this. And he could, finally, insist that whatever post-mortem states of affairs obtained, none of them, if expressible non-theistically, could suffice to verify any theistic claims. It is only this last position which is inconsistent with a doctrine of eschatological verification. But this last position is of course not moderate, but radical theological non-naturalism, which we have already seen reason to disregard as an irrational thesis. The other two responses are in no way inconsistent with some version of a doctrine of eschatological verification.

Let us now turn to the actual expectations which Hick places before us. He stresses, correctly, that mere survival of death would not serve to verify theism, since it might be a surprising natural fact and nothing more. What is needed to verify Christian theism is the experience of a community of persons whose relationship to one another represents the sort of fulfilment of human personality indicated in the Gospels, and who experience communion with God as revealed in

81

Christ. As these stand they seem to be references to states of affairs that could only form the subject-matter of theistic statements, rather than non-theistic ones. While I incline to read Hick otherwise, let us ask whether some predictions couched in non-theistic statements could have the same verificatory value. It is not too difficult to produce them. If we say that there will be a community of persons infused by grace, over whom Jesus will return to reign as the Son of God, we clearly make theistic statements. Suppose, however, that we confine ourselves to saying that there will be a community of persons whose personalities are as they *would be if* they were infused by grace (in that they manifest love, guilelessness, self-sacrifice, understanding, purity of heart); that Jesus will rule over this community as the Son of God *would* (in a manner manifesting these same personality-traits plus a uniquely high degree of knowledge, authority, forgiveness); and that the members of this predicted community think and behave as they do at least in part because they *consider themselves to be* infused by grace, to be redeemed sinners, to be children of one God whose Son has returned to rule over his kingdom. These statements are all non-theistic statements; they could be known to be true by someone who did not know that God existed. On the other hand, I would suggest that if someone were to find himself in a world in which these predictions turned out to have come true, he would be irrational if he did not take this as verifying the claims of Christian theism with which these predictions are associated.

An objection is natural here. It is natural to object that these predictions, even if non-theistic in the sense that someone could know them to be true without knowing that God existed, are theistic in another sense - that they could not be understood by someone who did not understand the claim that God exists, since they contain references to grace, redemption, and the Son of God. We might coin another technicality and say that any statement which cannot be understood by someone who does not *understand* the statement that God exists is a statement which 'contains theistic expressions'. Our discussion makes it seem very likely that any eschatological predictions which would be sufficient, if true, to verify the central claims of Christian theism, would be statements containing theistic expressions. But this is no objection to our claim that it is possible to state, in non-theistic statements, what post-mortem states of affairs would be sufficient to verify the central claims of Christian theism. It would only be an objection to a theory that was supposed to use the fact that such eschatological predictions can be made as a way of explaining the *meaning* of these central claims. In spite of quite explicit disclaimers, Hick has been criticised for allegedly trying to 'give meaning retrospectively' to Christian discourse by reference to a future crux(13). Such an enterprise would no doubt be circular, but it is neither Hick's nor ours. All that is claimed is that the predicted circumstances are of a sort that could be recognised to obtain by someone who did not know that God existed; not that they could be recognised to obtain by someone who did not understand the statement that God exists. I would suggest that the believer and the sceptic could and should agree that such a future world would verify the claims that Christians now make about God; that it would indeed be irrational to deny that it would. Although they could and should agree about this, it is very obvious that they will not agree about the likelihood of these things coming to pass, since one's estimate of such likelihood is dependent entirely upon whether or not one considers oneself already to have knowledge of God's existence and intentions. The sceptic here must take the position of the moderate theological non-naturalist.

A theological positivist can only deny the above argument in one of two ways. He can demand that the non-theistic statements which serve to verify theistic claims be statements that do not contain theistic expressions. This demand cannot be met, nor is it reasonable to expect it to be met. Alternatively, he can insist upon denying that the predicted situation would indeed suffice to verify Christian theism. This of course is a resort to radical theological non-naturalism, and is an irrational resort. It could only be supported by an insistence that one statement, q, can only suffice to verify another, p, if it entails it, an insistence that has only to be revealed to be exposed.

If all this is true, the doctrine of eschatological verification is successful, provided its objectives are properly defined.

Even if the descriptions of the verificatory post-mortem states of affairs have to be partly given in theistic statements, the doctrine would have shown that Christian theism makes claims which are in principle verifiable. But it does in fact seem possible to satisfy the stronger requirement that the theist be able to specify in non-theistic statements what would verify his claims - as long as these statements can include among them at least some that contain theistic expressions. So although the natural reaction of some theists to theological positivism is that its demands are unreasonable, and although no good reason has been given, *a priori*, for accepting these demands as necessary conditions of admitting the meaningfulness of religious discourse, it does not seem impossible for the theist to satisfy them. The price paid for this achievement is the recognition that the doctrine of eschatological verification cannot serve as a way of explaining how we are to understand talk of God. Even if we accept that such talk cannot be accorded meaning unless a mode of verification can be specified for it, it does not follow, and indeed cannot be admitted, that specifying its mode of verification is specifying what its meaning is.

In view of this result, we should conclude with a further independent comment on Flew's critique of theistic statements. In expounding it I distinguished two theses: the first, that believers do not seem to have different expectations from unbelievers; the second, that in consequence they empty the terms (like 'love') that they use to speak of God of all their ordinary meaning, since in ordinary contexts one applies these terms in statements that are verified or falsified by the satisfaction or frustration of expectations. These two criticisms have to be distinguished very clearly. The first is a demand to be told how the theist's claims about God can be verified or falsified. It is a reasonable demand, for, as Flew points out, religious vocabulary is untechnical. We speak of God in terms originally learned to speak of people. If these terms are being used in a way different from their non-religious use, some account of the religious use must be forthcoming. Since in their non-religious use statements containing them are verifiable or falsifiable, some analogue of the procedures of secular verification should be discernible. It would seem that

84

the doctrine of eschatological verification supplies this. But the second criticism is only partially answered by this move, since it also raises a much more fundamental difficulty about religious discourse, and a much older difficulty. The predicates applied to God, though familiar ones, are applied to a being declared to be infinitely different from ourselves: a being declared to be omnipotent, incorporeal, all-knowing, and the like. It follows from this that when such terms are applied to him many normal implications cannot be assumed. If God has knowledge, he cannot be said to learn. If God performs actions, he cannot do so as a result of making up his mind, and he cannot perform bodily movements. If God can be addressed, it is not because he has ears with which to hear us. It is partly because of this that so many procedures of secular verification are out of place. Because of the radical changes that ordinary predicates have to undergo when they are applied to God, and because of the radical human ignorance of God's nature which prevents us from knowing just how far this or that predicate applies, critics have often suggested, as Flew does, that the predicates we apply to God are emptied of their normal content and that nothing is supplied to replace it. This problem is only partly a problem to do with verification. Indeed, the problem of verification can only be met if one assumes that this other has an answer, so that statements containing theistic expressions can be understood. I have called it elsewhere the 'problem of the attenuation of religious predicates'(14). The doctrine of eschatological verification is not an answer to it. It was not even intended to be. But since Flew, in attacking religious discourse, did not distinguish these two problems clearly from one another, it has frequently been assumed by Flew's critics that it was intended to deal with it, though it manifestly cannot. None of our own discussions are attempts to deal with it either.

A final point of some consequence for Hick's theory: he suggests that verification may be confined to some specific group of people, and not be available to all. In particular, it might be that the verification of the claims of Christian theism is possible only for the faithful, and not for unbelievers(15). It is perhaps noteworthy that he expresses it by saying it might be that 'only the theistic believer can find the vindication of his belief'(16). The word 'vindication' is the natural one to use here: for the one who has all along proclaimed the truth of that which is now verified is indeed vindicated. What is not so clear, from our own earlier discussion, is that for this person his claims have been verified. If we are right in hesitating to admit that someone who knows that p can have p verified to or for him, then the only way of saying that the man of faith can have the tenets of his faith verified to him is to insist that he does not know them before. This is clearly not what Hick would wish, and in any case this is an inadequate reason for denying that faith can be knowledge. We have also seen, however, that someone who knows that p may be able to see that p is verified. Indeed, he may see this even when there is no one to or for whom it is verified. To have one's faith vindicated, then, may be to be in a position to see that it is verified, which entails that if there were someone who was aware of the verificatory facts but had hitherto hesitated to accept the tenets of the faith, that person would be acting irrationally if he then continued to refrain from accepting them. Doubt, however reasonable before, would not be reasonable now. It might of course be that sceptics were precluded from access to the states of affairs which served to verify the tenets of the faith, so that although the believer is vindicated, the unbeliever is not converted; in which case the faith is verified, but is not verified *to* anyone. Or it might be that the faith is verified to sceptics, but because of obstinacy they refuse to recognise that it has been. Which of these, or other, alternatives might come to pass is something on which independent authority is required.

This last difficulty arises because someone who knows something is the one who does not need to have it verified for him. But even if he is the only one who comes to see it has been verified, it does not follow from this that its being verified serves no purpose for him. For the knowledge that he has had all along might not have guided his conduct as much as it should; it might have been incomplete, fragmentary, and easily brushed aside under temptation, especially in a world where so many others denied it was knowledge at all. Just as proof can deepen knowledge, so the recognition that what one has known has now been verified may reinforce, for good, the hold which that knowledge has.

5 Revelation and Proof

(a) Faith and Scepticism

Let us begin with a brief summary. We have accepted, with appropriate reservations, the view that theistic statements cannot be proved from non-theistic premisses. We have seen reason to distinguish two versions of this view, named respectively moderate and radical theological non-naturalism. The moderate view states that there are no non-theistic premisses that we can know to be true which would serve to prove God's existence, or any other alleged theistic fact; but it allows that there might be some non-theistic statements which would serve to prove such conclusions if only they were known to be true. The radical view denies that there are any non-theistic statements whatever which, even if true, could prove such conclusions. We have argued that the radical view is an irrational view, so that both believers and sceptics should be able to agree upon some non-theistic premiss, or some set of non-theistic premisses, which, if true, would serve to prove some theistic conclusion without the further aid of theistic premisses. The choice of some set of non-theistic premisses as being probative ones would perhaps involve accepting an inference which sacrificed economy, and which added some degree of explanatory depth, but this loss and this gain would be incidental; the decision to regard such a set of premisses as probative could not be based upon a prior choice between these two considerations at a general level, since such a choice would lack justification unless critical substantive questions were begged. The probative force must be seen to lie in the examples themselves. To insist that no non-theistic premisses whatever could be probative is completely arbitrary unless it could be supported by independent demonstration of the incoherence of theism. It would not be enough merely to point out that the world as we find it does not supply us with probative facts; this would support moderate, but not radical, theological non-naturalism. Parallel considerations can be made out in the case of the verification of theistic claims. Here, even though there may be no non-theistic statements which we can know to be true which do put these claims beyond reasonable doubt, both believers and sceptics ought to be able to agree that certain situations, which could be described in non-theistic statements, would serve to do so. We have suggested that some of the eschatological predictions of the Christian tradition are, as John Hick has claimed, in this category. In both cases, however, the believer and the sceptic will take a different view of the likelihood of the probative or verificatory statements ever turning out to be true. This difference will be traceable to one source: the presence or absence of alleged independent knowledge of the truth of the religious claims. For someone without such knowledge only standard inductive considerations can be relevant to the question of the likelihood of any of the probative or verificatory statements coming true, and these considerations taken alone count firmly against them. For someone who considers himself to have this knowledge, a variety of possibilities are open. While he will be able to find proofs and verifications of theistic statements time and again by combining secular facts with religious ones he claims to know, he might take the same view the sceptic does about the likelihood of anything happening which would suffice to prove God's existence or God's love to those who do not know of it already (1). Many believers side with the sceptic over the likelihood of events occurring in this life which would suffice to prove any theistic conclusion without the aid of theistic premises. But most would take the opposite side from the sceptic on the eschatological predictions. In my own view, they ought to do so. They can, that is to say, be moderate theological non-naturalists about this world, but theological naturalists about the next: their alleged independent knowledge of God and his purposes would here override the inductive considerations to which the sceptic is confined, and which make him reject even the belief in survival of death, and would cause them to predict these fulfilments with confidence.

There is, then, or should be, an area of theoretical

agreement between believers and sceptics; but it is also obvious that on the practical level the deadlock is complete. For those who think they have independent knowledge of God will be able, by drawing upon this alleged knowledge, to construct a wholly rational and even systematic theocentric account of their world and their day-to-day affairs, which those who do not lay claim to this knowledge must, for this very reason, reject. This deadlock exists even though each side might agree both on what would make it irrational for the sceptic to continue to reject it, and on the fact that, this side of the grave, it will not be forthcoming. And it will exist even though each side might agree on what post-mortem situations would make it irrational to doubt the truth of theistic claims, since those who think they have independent knowledge of God and those who do not think they have are thereby enabled, without irrationality, to take quite different views of the likelihood of these post-mortem situations ever coming to pass. The theoretical assumptions that they may share are not sufficient, it seems, to allow useful debate between them on the basis of agreed standards. Each must see the world differently, one as God's world and the other as not. The naturalness of this form of words here gives a strong initial plausibility to Hick's attempt to account for the nature of the believer's stance (his faith) in the language of 'seeing-as'. We are approaching, but have not yet reached, the stage where the adequacy of this notion for this purpose can be judged.

Can this deadlock be broken down? In a way it certainly can, because it often is. People are converted: those who do not have the alleged independent knowledge of God come to believe that they do have it; and people who used to think they had it change their minds about its genuineness. But this is not the outcome of debate according to agreed standards. For if we are right that there are no indirect proofs now to be had, conversion will be a process of inducing in someone the religious insight that he so far lacks. Doing this to someone is usually a matter of preaching to him. If one has theistic knowledge, or considers oneself to have it, then no doubt one is correct in interpreting what happens when a man is preached at as being a process of revealing to him what he has so far not seen, by putting him in a position where he can see

89

it. But if one is sceptical of the truth of theistic claims and judges them by the standards one would use for assessing procedures that lead to knowledge in areas where one does claim to know something, it is clear that preaching has then to appear as a set of dubious persuasive devices designed to cloud the judgement and induce belief by putting aside normal requirements of objectivity - devices to which the rational man would not submit any more than he would to mob oratory. Similarly, the attempts to convince believers that their alleged insights are illusory, even if they work, seem bound to commit the 'genetic fallacy'(2) and to depend on applying to religious beliefs standards which those who hold them can quite rationally insist do not apply to them. A familiar example of this, that will shortly concern us, is the continual debate about the cognitive significance of religious experience. No amount of psychological knowledge of the genesis of such experience can (or should) show to someone who considers himself to know of God's presence that such experience cannot be revelatory, yet no amount of insistence that it is a form of cognition can (or should) convince someone who does not think he knows of God's presence that it really is. No community of standards exists which would enable the kind of agreement we have argued to be possible about imagined cases, to be arrived at for the experience that the world in fact does offer. The deadlock is deepened by the fact that the believer and the unbeliever each has at his disposal, if he wishes to use them, explanatory devices for accounting for the alleged blindness or gullibility of the other (3).

To say that the deadlock is complete in practice, then, is to say that even though the transition from scepticism to faith or faith to scepticism is common enough, there is no non-question-begging way of describing such transition or, at least, of attempting to justify it. Here it is natural to protest that such a position neglects the claims that believers make for revelation. Certainly the critical place that the notion of independent knowledge of God has in our previous account requires that some examination of this vexed concept now be attempted.

90

(b) The Concept of Revelation

Both those Christians who have thought that Christian doctrines could in part be proved and those who have not thought so have agreed that Christianity is a revealed religion. What have they meant by this claim? It is immediately clear that anyone who says that there has been, or is, a revelation of God is making a theistic statement. Sceptics cannot be said to know that there is a revelation, any more than they can be said to know that men are sinners, or that Christ was the Son of God. What they can do, of course, is agree that there have been, or are, alleged revelations. In order to maintain philosophical neutrality in discussing revelation, we must confine ourselves to an account of the concept without commenting on the question of whether or not there are any instances of it - that is, any actual revelations. I shall confine my discussion in this way.

It is important, however, that the sceptic can agree that there are alleged revelations. For this means not only that there are people who have alleged that there have been revelations. It also means that there have been phenomena which believers have claimed to be revelatory ones. In other words, a sceptic who denies that x is, as the believer claims, a revelation of God, need not question that x has occurred, though he may. He need only question whether the believer is interpreting its significance correctly. I shall confine my considerations primarily to cases where he does not deny it has occurred (4).

Christians have divided over what is revealed, and over what form the revelation of it takes. They have divided on the first question into those who have held that revelation is of propositions, and those who have held that revelation is of God himself. They have divided on the second question into those who have held that revelation is in the form of persons and events, and those who have held it is in the form of authoritative pronouncements. These are only very rough divisions, especially the second, and there are other divisions also, such as the division over whether or not revelations ceased at some date or still continue. I shall try to avoid a conceptual account that appears to take sides between these positions.

Let us look at the first dispute, which was touched upon briefly in Chapter 1. It is sufficient for present purposes to re-emphasise what was said there. St Thomas, usually taken as the classical exponent of the propositional view of revelation, still says that the ultimate object of faith is God himself. Conversely, even if one holds that it is God who is revealed, and not propositions about God, this cannot be rendered intelligible in a form which does not entail that the person to whom God is revealed is thereby made aware of some critical truths about God. This is shown from the fact that the appropriate responses to revelation thus described (submission, gratitude, and the like) are all attitudes that one cannot have without also having certain beliefs about their object. No doubt the non-propositional view of revelation allows for much more doctrinal elasticity in the interpretation of the revelatory events, since there is more than one belief which could supply a sufficient reason for gratitude or submission; but this merely shows that there can be more *mis*interpretations of revelation on this view of revelation than on the other. So it seems that, on both views, someone who claims that a particular event or action or pronouncement is revelatory is at least claiming that through it he and others are enabled to know some truth about God, whatever else he claims. If we turn now to the second dispute, we can avoid taking sides in it also. For what is critical for our purposes is the recognition that whether the revelation is in the form of some human action, or event, or pronouncement, there is some revelatory phenomenon that takes place, or is present, and can be recognised to have done so whether or not it is agreed to be revelatory. In our own terminology, to interpret some action or event or pronouncement as revelatory is to take some phenomenon that can be reported in non-theistic statements and to claim that it can also enable us to know the truth of some theistic statement. Some fact is alleged to be significant beyond itself, to be what it is 'and more' (5).

That which is taken to be revelatory may be something which can only be reported in statements containing theistic expressions. For example, anyone who denies that the visions of Joan of Arc or Bernadette were revelatory, but does not deny that they had them, must say that they had visions of

St Catherine or of the Virgin, but that they were not authentic. In saying this they will be making non-theistic statements that contain theistic expressions. This is bound to happen whenever it is impossible to report the allegedly revelatory event accurately without stating that someone involved in it had certain beliefs about what was happening to him or her; and purported visions are in this category. On the other hand, many allegedly revelatory events appear susceptible of description without the use of theistic expressions. Some, for example, may think the capture of Jerusalem by Israel in 1967 to be in some way revelatory of God's care for his people; but whether or not it is, it clearly can be, and was, reported in sentences containing wholly non-theistic expressions. Other allegedly revelatory events, such as the Exodus, could only be reported in wholly non-theistic expressions with great effort, since the beliefs that the Jews held about what was taking place themselves played their part in the development of the event, and the beliefs were beliefs about God and his relationship to them. But this is a side-issue. Whether the revelatory phenomena can or cannot be reported in sentences containing no theistic expressions, they can be reported in non-theistic statements. It is a matter of history that certain events occurred, that certain actions were done, that certain pronouncements were made. Someone can know that they occurred, were done, or were made, whether or not he knows that God exists. If he claims that these phenomena are revelations of God, then he is claiming not only that they have taken place, but, in addition, that they show us some fact about God.

Let us suppose that some revelatory event is reported in the non-theistic statement, p. Let us suppose that what it reveals to us is stated in the theistic statement, q. The sceptic can assert p, but must reject q. The believer asserts both. Complex questions face us when we ask what else can be said about the relationship between p and q. The believer, in calling the fact that p revelatory, is committed to the view that at least some men have been placed in a position to know that q by being placed in a position to know that p. This is extremely vague, and its vagueness is not lessened when one reflects that it is doctrinally impossible for him to say that it is only through being placed in a position to know

93

that p that anyone could be in a position to know that q; for God can reveal himself, presumably, when and how he chooses. One fact, however, is clear enough. It is that it need not be irrational for someone who does not know that God exists to accept p and reject q, even if p is revelatory of q. The claim that p is revelatory of q, in other words, is consistent with moderate theological non-naturalism. For the latter is a doctrine about what would prove or verify theistic statements. In this respect at least revelation differs from both proof and verification. If this were not the case, the theological non-naturalist would be forced to deny that any revelation ever occurs, for if it were to occur it would also provide adequate subject-matter for the premiss of a proof of what is revealed.

In the history of religious thought, however, we are not just accustomed to a *distinction* between revelation and proof. We are used to a *contrast* between them. How can this be made out? I submit that it can only be made out partially at best. Let us suppose that our non-theistic statement p, which, *ex hypothesi*, we know to be true, either entails or renders overwhelmingly probable the theistic statement, q. This would make it both probative and revelatory. Theological non-naturalism requires the denial of the occurrence of probative revelations, simply because it denies the occurrence of probative non-theistic facts. But if there are revelations, why can there not be probative ones? Why could there not be phenomena which are reportable in non-theistic statements, which reveal to men truths which are only expressible in theistic statements, and which could also serve as the premisses of proofs of those theistic statements? I can detect no incoherence in this suggestion, even if prior acceptance of theological non-naturalism makes us reject all proofs from non-theistic statements, and therefore, *a fortiori*, probative revelations. Given that the epistemic process of revelation is not the same as the epistemic process of proof, there seems no reason in logic why they should not, now and again, overlap, by involving the same phenomena.

The suggestion may seem disturbing, in view of the conventional wisdom, common to Catholic and Protestant, which tells us that proof and revelation are exclusive. If we are prepared to question the parallel contrast between faith and knowledge, we ought to be prepared to scrutinise this one also.

(a) It might be said that if some theistic statement could be proved from some non-theistic premiss, there would then be no need for the same truth to be revealed, especially through the very same fact. But this has only to be said to be seen to be questionable. The need might very well arise from the nature of the audience. St Thomas says that some truths about God that can be known by proof are also made available to men through revelation because not all men are capable of the labour and intellectual discernment needed to follow the proofs. We have seen reason to question his additional thesis that only those who have these truths proved to them can know them, but we can agree to what he says about the need for the others to learn of them some other way. For even if it would be irrational to reject our theistic statement, q, for someone who knows the truth of our non-theistic statement, p, and can see its probative force, it does not follow that everyone who knows that p is clever enough to discern that p makes q overwhelmingly probable. (He may not even be able to state p and q sufficiently clearly for us to be certain that he distinguishes them from one another.) This need not prevent him from learning that q by learning that p. Someone who is able to discern their relationship could perhaps have one mode of cognition reinforced by the other.

(b) A further fact should make us more receptive to the concept of a probative revelation. St Thomas held that assent to revealed truths was reasonable in the light of the prior acceptance of the results of natural theology. Even though we cannot presuppose such results, a clear truth remains in his contention. We have already seen that someone who considers himself to know of the existence of God is in a position to construct many entirely sound proofs using God's existence, and any other prior knowledge of God he has, in the premisses, and combining with this some other non-theistic premiss. The man whose knowledge is confined to what can be stated non-theistically cannot do this. This has a present application. Even believers are not always certain whether or not some event or experience is revelatory. In trying to decide this, they consider it in the

95

light of other knowledge of God that they consider themselves to possess. In some cases, given the existence of this prior knowledge, it would be unreasonable not to hold that what is alleged to be revealed by some event or pronouncement, is. Given, for example, what the Roman Catholic Church claims to know about the authority vested in the Papacy, it is unreasonable to deny those dogmas proclaimed through papal pronouncements; and to accept them on these grounds is to accept the revelatory character of those pronouncements. Given what Catholic and Protestant alike have claimed to know about the person of Christ, it is unreasonable, if one accepts that Christ washed the feet of his disciples, not to recognise this as an act designed to teach men how to behave towards one another, and to agree that this is what it is for these reasons is to agree that the act is revelatory. But in both these cases it is equally clear that the prior theistic knowledge could, if one wished, be presented as a major premiss, the pronouncement or act as a minor premiss, and the theological or moral truth as the conclusion, of a successful proof. This is a slightly formalised presentation of the way a good deal of theology proceeds, and we have already had occasion to draw attention to it. So although the concepts of proof and revelation are distinct, it would be very strange if they were exclusive, for this would prevent us from subsuming one and the same phenomenon under both headings.

(c) We might well wonder in these circumstances why the traditional contrast between proof and revelation has been so sharply drawn, and why it should have seemed so persuasive. One reason has already been hinted at. Even though a revelatory fact can be reported in non-theistic statements, and therefore in a way that does not place a religious interpretation upon it, it does not follow from this that the person or persons for whom this fact is revelatory have any occasion to make the necessary separation, or even have the ability to do so. It is more likely to be the sceptic who insists upon such a separation, and says, for example, that the believer has had an experience which he *took to be* a vision of the Virgin, or witnessed an event which he *took to be* the fulfilment of a divine promise. But even though those who take themselves to have received revelation may not make such a separation, it will still be true that the phenomenon that has served as a revelation for them is identifiable independently of this fact: that there has indeed been some experience or event which they have taken to be revelatory, as the sceptic has said. He is right in this, even if he is wrong in holding that they ought not to have taken it in the way they have. If the separation is not made in practice, then the phenomenon will not be described in a way which enables it to be used to launch an attempted proof from non-theistic premisses; and someone who considers himself to have learned of God through it is likely to be so preoccupied with what the phenomenon *also* is, that he will not be concerned to separate out some antiseptic account of what it minimally is. The further back we go in the history of the Judaeo-Christian tradition, the less we find men who have intellectual occasion to separate their secular from their religious knowledge in this manner. The man who considers that God is revealing something of himself to him through some event or experience is not necessarily considering that the event or experience is a *reason for believing* that which is revealed. But this does not create any logical barrier to someone's offering it as a reason - indeed, as the premiss of a proof. Such arguments are by no means unknown. It is this sort of argument that is the target of Hume's critique in his essay on 'Miracles', at least on the most likely interpretation. Hume is attacking those who attempt to establish theistic conclusions on the basis of statements reporting miraculous occurrences. These could be stated non-theistically, but were thought to provide proof of theistic conclusions. Hume undermines arguments of this form by finding what are, in his view, conclusive independent reasons for rejecting the non-theistic premisses of such arguments (6). But the miracle stories apologists might take to provide such premisses are stories of events which would be classed by those who believe them as revelatory events. So there have been at least some cases where apologists have implied that one and the same phenomenon can be stated non-theistically and be both probative and revelatory.

(d) Although certain phenomena are singled out as revelatory in some central or normative manner, any phenomenon may be classed as revelatory of God. Many of those that would be so classed could not be construed, even by the most zealous of natural theologians, as probative also, even though there is no logical difficulty in holding that something may be both. Some of the central revelatory phenomena of the Christian tradition are of a sort that do not appear in the premisses of proofs. One reason for this, to which we will return, is the fact that they are alleged historical events, and even if they were agreed to be of the kind which would prove theistic conclusions if they were known to be true, doubts have been raised about whether they actually occurred, so that sceptics could always insist that the premisses of proofs starting from them were not known to be true. This is one obvious reason why natural theologians have used as premisses of their proofs not the stories of the miraculous that Hume attacks, but statements of the utterly familiar. What, for example, could be more undeniable than St Thomas's premiss in the First Way: 'It is certain, and evident to our senses, that in the world some things are in motion.' The preference for premisses of this kind is due less to their generality than to the fact that they are undeniably known; the difficulty about historical premisses is not their particularity, but the fact that they are so easy to doubt. It is worthy of note that some natural theologians, daunted but not defeated by criticisms of the traditional arguments, have tried to salvage something from their wreck by suggesting that even though they may not be successful proofs, they may still be successful in inducing a particular apprehension of finite things - as dependent on a self-existent creator, or as manifesting design (7). Such an apprehension can be induced in someone without formal argumentation; and it can be induced in someone by a discourse which appears to be an argument, but which lacks the relationships between premisses and conclusion which are necessary for a successful proof. I have argued at length elsewhere that the traditional arguments are indeed attempts to induce such an apprehension, misleadingly disguised as demonstrations (8). The truth in such attempts to defend them lies in the fact that the very familiar phenomena from which they begin can be found revelatory. No doubt reflecting on the proofs is one way of preparing one's mind to recognise them to be revelatory, if they are. What is thought of as probative but is not may be revelatory nevertheless, and what is bad proof may be good preaching.

(c) Revelation and Response

The upshot of these considerations is that the distinction between revelation and proof is clear, and the contrast between revelation and proof is natural; but nothing makes it logically absurd to suggest that there might be phenomena that can be known to obtain by believer and sceptic alike, that would suffice to provide the premises of the proof of some theistic conclusion, and were revelatory also. A theological non-naturalist would have to deny that such phenomena in fact obtained, or are known to have obtained, but he could agree that if they had they would be sufficient to prove some theistic conclusion. I have called such possible phenomena probative revelatory phenomena.

Before returning to assess the importance of this possibility, let us investigate the concept of revelation further in general. The notion of a revelatory phenomenon is vague. The vagueness has been deliberate, since it has been part of my contention that the points I have attempted to make are sound whichever side a reader might take in some of the traditional disputes about revelation. I have argued that whether revelation is of propositions about God or of God himself, it must yield some propositional knowledge about God if it ever occurs. I have also argued that whether that which is revelatory is a set of statements in a book, or a series of pronouncements by a person, or a historical event, or the history of a nation, or the life of a man, or a single human act, it is still possible to distinguish between that which is found to be revelatory and that which it reveals. The former will be identifiable in principle by common or scientific observation, or by historical investigation, or by report. These two minimal claims are consistent with all the major competing views of what revelation is, and they enable us to hold that it is always possible in principle to describe that which is held to be revelatory in a non-theistic way, and therefore in a way which the sceptic can agree to. It is of course impossible to express the alleged knowledge which is revealed through it in anything but theistic statements, and these the sceptic will reject. In spite of these common features, allegedly revelatory phenomena vary very widely; and it is far from true that one either accepts them all as revelatory or rejects them all. Believers accept some and reject others, and will disagree over the interpretation to be accorded to this one or that; and it is possible not only for a believer to be unsure whether or not some phenomenon is revelatory, but for an unbeliever to be hesitant too. Examples of these kinds of disagreement are easy to find. The life and pronouncements of Joseph Smith are accepted by a considerable number as revelatory, but many more reject them. The claims of the Roman Church to be the vehicle of continuing revelation are accepted by millions, and rejected by millions. Although the story of the Last Supper is agreed by all Christians to have revelatory significance, there is wide disagreement over what significance it has. One interesting area of dispute arises in the interpretation of some religious experiences: it is tempting to say that no one can have certain kinds of religious experience and fail to interpret them theistically - much as it is tempting to say that no one could feel pain of a certain intensity without showing signs of distress; it seems absurd, for example, to say that St Paul on the road to Damascus, or St Teresa, might have had the same experiences that have been reported to us, but might have given them a different interpretation. This does not show that their interpretations were true, or that others could not report that Paul or Teresa had these experiences, and report them in non-theistic statements. (Not, of course, in non-theistic expressions.) It is consequently unprofitable linguistic legislation, even though it is tempting, to insist that all genuine religious experiences must be given theistic interpretations by those who have them. R. W. Hepburn, for example, has suggested that the much-discussed numinous experience may be had, and even be cultivated, by the unbeliever, even though it has been one of the deepest sources of a theistic apprehension of the world, since it is possible to have it yet refrain from giving it the theistic interpretation that it is natural to accord to it (9). I would hesitate to join H. D. Lewis in questioning the logical possibility of such a sophisticated separation of an experience and its interpretation (10). Even if we insisted that a strong

100

or deep numinous experience is necessarily not one that someone can have without believing himself to be in the presence of God, it is still quite clear that someone's having such an experience, belief and all, is something that can be reported by someone else without entailing that the belief that is part of it is a true one.

Some critics of religion have suggested that there is a logical absurdity about claims made by believers to have experienced God, or to have acquired knowledge of God through having certain experiences. Such criticisms may have force against claims that the occurrence of any phenomenon, including certain religious experience, is a guarantee of the truth of a theistic interpretation of it, unless one such phenomenon is a probative one, for such a claim is probably due, in our terminology, to a suggestion that what cannot be reported without theistic expressions has to be reported in theistic statements, and this is a muddle. A natural theology based on religious experience is likely to fare no better than any other form of natural theology. But this does not show that the experience of some phenomenon may not in fact be revelatory of God; merely that it does not have to be interpreted in this way.

When and if revelation does occur, however, there is some phenomenon, reportable in non-theistic statements, which is such as to enable someone to know something that would provide the content for a theistic statement. The preceding has been expressed in language reminiscent of our earlier discussions of proof and verification. Let us explore further to see how far the analogy between revelation and proof will go, and where it breaks down. In what follows I shall, in order to avoid tiresomeness, refrain from indicating the religious neutrality of this argument every time the word 'revelation' is used. Where necessary, the reader should add such a clause as 'if revelation ever occurs'.

The speaker-hearer distinction is clearly present in the case of revelation, as it is in the case of proof. But the 'speaker' is always identical, namely God himself. That is to say, it is always God who is said to make himself, or propositions about himself, known, using revelatory events or pronouncements as instruments. The hearer is sometimes spoken of by theologians as being the whole of mankind, or

101

some generation or class of men; but it is usually taken to be individuals. It seems clear that the hearer or hearers have to know that the revelatory phenomenon has occurred for anything thereby to have been revealed to them (11). But much more difficult questions arise when we ask whether, for revelation to occur, the hearer has to see the import of the revelatory phenomenon; and whether he has to know the truth of the theistic statements that state that which is revealed before it can be true that the revelation has been given him. It would be utopian to expect theological literature to yield clear answers to these questions, since so many doctrinal disputes are involved in answering them. I shall hazard some tentative arguments.

It is necessary for any account of the concept of revelation to allow for the fact that revelation can be rejected. It must be possible to state that someone has understood what import the allegedly revelatory phenomenon would have, but denies that to which it points. Furthermore, such denial, given our earlier comments that the revelatory phenomena can be reported non-theistically, need not be irrational for someone who does not have knowledge of God already. The difference here between the definition of proof and that of revelation is fundamental, since the irrationality of rejection is part of the concept of proof. In the case of revelation, rejection would be irrational for someone who had prior knowledge of God, if that prior knowledge, together with the knowledge of the occurrence of the revelatory phenomenon, made some theistic conclusion overwhelmingly probable, and the hearer was in a position to recognise all this. Self-deception in the face of some revelatory phenomenon could arise in the same sort of situation. If anyone wished to hold that all rejection of revelation is irrational, or involves self-deception, he would minimally have to postulate such prior knowledge of God in all unbelievers. He would have to say that all men in fact know enough of God prior to the revelation to know very well that it is a revelation (12).

Whether or not all rejection of revelation is in this category, someone who rejects some theistic claim while being aware of the occurrence of the allegedly revelatory phenomenon, but does this without being cognisant that the phenomenon might have revelatory import, is not someone to whom anything has been revealed through that phenomenon. But someone who sees what import it would have and rejects it nevertheless might still have had something revealed to him. (This does not mean that the one for whom there has not been a revelation is blameless. It might be that his inability to grasp the revelatory import of the phenomenon he knows about is the result of a life devoted to sensual pursuits or the search for financial security or power, which has dulled his capacity to notice the significance of what happens around him.)

These considerations suggest the following tentative results. For a revelation to occur, the revelatory phenomenon has to be known to have occurred by at least one person able to see what its import is; but it is not necessary that this person should accept it. Like proof, revelation is person-relative: there has to be someone to whom that which is revealed, is revealed. But that person, though necessarily able to see what the revelatory phenomenon points to, may not accept that to which it points. Furthermore, unless there are probative revelations, his rejection cannot be classed as irrational or the outcome of self-deception if he lacks prior knowledge of God.

If this is sound, a common theological manoeuvre is misguided. This is the decision so to define the word 'revelation' that revelation can only be said to have occurred when it has been accepted. Let us look, for example, at the following quotation from John Baillie:

> We must, however, think very carefully what we mean when we say that revelation is given in the form of events or historical happenings. For it is not as if all who experience these events and happenings find in them a revelation of God. The question thus arises as to whether such events as are in themselves 'mighty acts of God' can properly be spoken of as revelation, if, in fact, there should be nobody to whom they reveal anything. To take the human analogy, do all my efforts to make myself plain amount to a real self-disclosure, if none succeeds in grasping what is in my mind? Surely not. We must therefore say that the receiving is as necessary to a completed act of revelation as the giving. It is only so far

as the action of God in history is understood as God means
it to be understood that revelation has place at all.(13)

The difficulty is that this prevents us from saying that revelation can be rejected, and leaves us without a name for that
which is rejected when such rejection occurs. Of course such
a decision is not *wrong*: one can use a word as one chooses.
But the disadvantage is clear. The manoeuvre is understandable and instructive, however. (i) We have seen that
there is excellent reason to insist that revelation cannot occur
without someone's being aware of what the allegedly revelatory phenomenon might portend. (ii) It is very natural to feel
a special difficulty about the recognition of revelatory
phenomena if these are held to include historical events
rather than proclamations, as they clearly are in this quotation. A proclamation carries its import on its face: the only
question is whether what is proclaimed to be so is so or not.
An event, on the other hand, has to be interpreted, and many
men will miss the interpretation - will, indeed, not see that
the event could have any significance beyond itself at all.
Some 'uptake' is necessary, and this is necessarily in the mind
of the beholder of the event, or of him who hears of it. But
this is not sufficient reason to conflate the beholder's recognition that it may have transcendent significance from his
decision that it does or does not (14). (iii) Many theologians
would wish to emphasise that the acceptance of a revelation
is something for which a man ought not to take credit himself, but should ascribe to God's grace. This makes it tempting
to treat the revelatory phenomenon and the acceptance of it
as one divine action. This is of course difficult to hold along-
side any view that rejection is blameworthy, even if we do
have some word to use to name that which is rejected. But
aside from this problem, the claim that the acceptance is due
to God, if intended to imply that it is not also a free action
on the man's part, entails a doctrine of election which requires independent theological justification and should not
gain acceptance through the mere decision to define revelation so that God's provision of a revelatory phenomenon and
a man's acceptance of it are not distinguishable. If the claim
is not so intended, then we have an implicit admission that
the two need to be distinguished, even though God is given

ultimate credit for both.

Closely related to this issue of the relation between revelation and the response to it is the question: how far apart in time and space can the revelatory phenomenon and the recognition of it be? If we insist that revelation can only occur if that which is revelatory is known to at least one person who can see its import, we have to admit the logical possibility that a revelatory phenomenon might occur at one time but not be recognised until many years afterwards: better, that it might not become revelatory until many years afterwards. This issue can perhaps be overlooked in the case of the alleged revelatory events recorded in the gospels, for even though they are held to be revelatory for succeeding generations, they are also held to have been revelatory at the time, whether accepted or whether rejected. It certainly seems possible, however, that some event, well known at the time of its occurrence but not seen to have transcendent import at that time, might be seen in retrospect to have it by those who learn about it in later generations; as when Christians claim to see signs of God's providence in the records of the history of pagan societies. It also seems possible that some natural phenomenon that has remained quite unknown to men for millions of years should serve as a revelation to those who eventually discover it. The possibility of a wide separation in time and space between a revelatory phenomenon and the awareness of it is of most consequence in theologies that distinguish sharply between a revelation and the record of it, or witness to it. If the Scriptures are themselves considered to be the revelation of God, for example, they are not physically or temporally separated from their readers. If, on the other hand, they are themselves merely records of certain events, and it is the events themselves that are the revelatory phenomena, we are forced to say that a revelatory event can occur at one time and be revelatory at innumerable other times, unless we insist that the events are only revelatory for those present at them. So the records and subsequent proclamations are, as it were, the ancillary vehicles that enable those in later generations to respond to the earlier events. One could of course say both that the events are revelatory and that the records, or the proclamations, are also revelatory. This latter need not imply that the record or the proclamation is infallibly accurate in all details. The tendency to refrain from admitting that the records or the later proclamations can themselves be revelatory usually derives from a Protestant insistence on the unique and definitive character of the primary revelatory events of the tradition (15).

Whichever view one adopts on these matters, two decisions have to be taken. (i) Believers and unbelievers alike will be faced by claims that some phenomena are revelatory, and they will be unsure how to assess these claims in certain cases. The believer, who will admit that some phenomena are revelatory but is perplexed about claims made for others, will treat certain allegedly revelatory phenomena as normative, and will evaluate the claims made for the others in the light of the import of the normative ones. The decisions on which are normative and which are not are the decisions which, above all others, divide the sects of Christendom from one another. (ii) Even with regard to the normatively revelatory phenomena some men will be unsure. Apart from the most general of all grounds for hesitation, i.e. doubt as to whether any theistic statements whatever are true, there is one very obvious ground for rational doubt over many claims that one hears: concern over whether the allegedly revelatory phenomenon ever occurred. This concern can arise when one is confronted with the claim that a scriptural document is itself revelatory, since someone doubtful of this claim might well want to know before assessing it whether or not the events told of in the document actually happened. But the problem appears most clearly of all when the claim is that some revelatory events took place in the remote past. Here a waverer may agree that if the events indeed occurred they would have been revelations from God; but this would justify his wishing for better than average assurances that the events in question did happen. We have Hume to remind us, once more, that there are major epistemological disadvantages in our traditional dependence upon oral tradition and witnesses. This prompts a question: is this particular disadvantage not theologically gratuitous? I shall return to this difficulty shortly.

(d) Revelation and Proof

Let us now look again at the epistemological deadlock that divides the believer and the unbeliever. In most cases the believer will hold that the knowledge of God which he considers himself to have, and which the unbeliever lacks, is the fruit of revelation. It is clear that no resolution of the deadlock as we described it can come from an appeal to revelation, since it is not irrational for someone lacking such independent knowledge to reject the believer's interpretation of any allegedly revelatory phenomenon. Perhaps it is irrational for someone possessing such knowledge, or considering himself to do so, to reject such claims in certain cases, but this does not speak to the deadlock that divides the believer and the unbeliever; at most it speaks to divisions between one group of believers and another. In such a situation the believer can only continue to proclaim the revelatory character of those phenomena that are central to his faith, in the hope that, as he sees the matter, the sceptic will one day come to see their real significance and accept that to which they point: he must, in simpler words, continue to preach. But since the phenomena he points to when he preaches are not probative phenomena, it is not irrational to reject the interpretation he places upon them, and the sceptic, with his epistemic limitations, is justified in rejecting the vision of things thus presented to him, whether he finds it seductive or whether he finds it repellent. So while the appeal to revelation may in fact convert, it does not, once again, do anything to bring about a consensus through an appeal to agreed standards, and the deadlock is as complete as before.

Must we therefore conclude that the gulf cannot be bridged? If theological non-naturalism, even in its moderate version, is true, we must. Let us rehearse the situation again. Even though there are no non-theistic statements which we can know to be true which are sufficient to prove the truth of theistic claims, believers and sceptics can, or should, agree that certain non-theistic statements would suffice to do so if only they were known to be true. This follows, as is familiar, from the irrationality of radical theological non-naturalism. At least as regards this life, the same area of agreement ought to exist about non-theistic statements that would verify the

107

claims that the theist makes. But without any expectation of the probative non-theistic statements becoming true, or of any inconsistency being demonstrated in theism, neither side can convince the other without passing beyond the area of theoretical agreement. We can state this predicament more succinctly: given the incontestable fact that Christianity is a revealed religion, and given the truth of theological non-naturalism, disagreement between believers and sceptics cannot be due to failure to meet standards agreed upon by both sides; and the standards appealed to by one side to criticise the stance of the other will be question-begging.

But why did we espouse theological non-naturalism in the first place? Because the world as we know it does not appear to be one that provides us with probative phenomena, even if it provides us, as believers think, with revelatory phenomena. If the world did provide us with probative phenomena, then those who, knowing of them, rejected the believer's claims, could be convicted of irrationality, and the deadlock would be resolved. The number of unbelievers might be no less than it is, but their unbelief could be condemned by standards that they themselves must espouse.

Probative phenomena *per se* would do nothing for those who cannot follow proofs based upon them; hence the need for revelation, even if proofs abound. But without probative phenomena rejection is always justifiable, and never without excuse. What would serve, if only it occurred, to retain the character of Christianity as a revealed religion, and yet to break the epistemological deadlock I have attempted to describe?

The answer is simple: a phenomenon that could be known to obtain, that could be reported in non-theistic statements, that would serve as a revelation of God, and would also serve to put some theistic conclusion beyond rational doubt. I have called this a probative revelatory phenomenon, and have stressed its logical possibility. In the tradition it has another more familiar name: a sign. A sign is that which reveals God and which it would be irrational to reject. If theological non-naturalism is true, of course, no sign will occur; for no proofs will. The sceptic, committed as he is to theological non-naturalism, does not expect a sign, whether or not he wishes for one. Believers who espouse theological non-naturalism do not expect signs either. Indeed the world does not seem to provide them. But if a sign would break the deadlock, what reason can the believer suggest for a probative revelatory phenomenon's never occurring? Several come to mind, but we have already seen enough to reject them.

(i) He might argue that a sign would compel assent, and that God does not compel assent. But if a sign is a probative phenomenon, this would not compel assent. It would merely ensure that rejection was the result of irrationality or self-deception on the part of those in a position to realise the probative force of it. Free agents can be irrational and can deceive themselves, and no doubt would continue to do this whatever the world were like. It should perhaps be noted again that proving something to someone is not the same as frightening him into believing it.

(ii) He might say that whatever sign God gave, men would not accept it. 'If they hear not Moses and the prophets, neither will they be persuaded, though one rose from the dead' (Luke 16:31). What is at issue, however, is not what men will allow themselves to be persuaded by. It is what it would be unreasonable for them to reject. Perhaps men without signs may have discreditable motives for requesting evidence of the quality that only a sign could provide, but this does not take away the fact that if a sign were provided for them they would then have no good reasons to cling to in order to justify their refusal, whereas without one they do have good reasons (16).

(iii) He might argue that if men were furnished with signs there would be no need for faith. This must mean that those who come to know of God through some phenomenon that proves him to them have no need for faith; for most would not learn of him through proofs at any time, even if they were available. But this is only plausible if we insist that faith and proof are incompatible, and we have already seen reason to doubt this.

The question remains: what theological reason can there be for insisting that the rejection of Christian claims must not only be free, but must also be reasonable? If God does not exist, it follows that nothing will prove that he does. If he does exist, it does not follow that anything will prove that he does; but in that case does it not follow instead that there must be a morally adequate reason why nothing will prove this? The above arguments do not show that no such reason can exist, but they throw doubt on the most familiar ones. Perhaps the readiness of many latter-day believers to accept theological non-naturalism is unwise. The absence of good proofs makes such an acceptance look like a practical necessity, but it is doubtful whether a theological virtue can be made of it also.

A final consideration before we return to the nature of faith. Someone might say that Christianity rests its claims upon just such phenomena as those just considered; that the gospel story, culminating in the Resurrection, gives just the probative revelatory phenomena which would supply an answer to our difficulty. But this has a serious difficulty of its own. If the gospel records are true, the events they record are indeed (I would submit) both probative and revelatory. But are these records true? We have already touched upon the problem of relating a revelatory episode to the response to it, where the two are widely separated in time. What concerns us here is how this can affect a phenomenon's probative character, rather than its revelatory character. A necessary condition of such a phenomenon's serving to prove to someone that some theistic conclusion is true is that the hearer should know the phenomenon to have occurred. And the fact that it is only the reports of witnesses that are before him makes this something which it is always rational to dispute - at least for someone without prior theistic knowledge. The difficulty is multiplied many times, as Hume saw, when what the witnesses tell of is something miraculous, which there is always good general reason to think does not occur. The probative status of the primary events of the tradition, given the person-relativity of proof, is therefore confined to those who witnessed the events (or those who have other theistic knowledge which makes it irrational to doubt that they occurred as recorded). For others, the deadlock appears to remain. To remove it a sign would be needed for each generation. Such a sign need not detract from the unique doctrinal centrality of the primary events; for the sign could be some phenomenon which showed it to be unreasonable to question the historicity, or authority, or import, of the primary events - by proving, for example, the authority of the contemporary

110

who proclaimed them, or the authenticity of the documents that bore witness to them, or the likeness of the deity to what was proclaimed in those documents about him. So a contemporary sign need not be such as to supersede the primary revelatory status of the gospel events; it could rather help to establish it for those separated from those events by so many years. Perhaps as many would turn aside as ever; but they would be stripped of their excuses for doing so. Why should they not be?

6 Faith

(a) Philosophical Understanding and Religious Faith

The primary purpose of this volume has been that of delineating the epistemological disagreement that divides
believers from unbelievers, and of deciding how far agreement between them is possible, and how far not. The
secondary purpose has been that of coming to a partial
understanding of the nature of faith, since it is faith that the
believer has and the sceptic does not have, and faith, therefore, that we have been describing, by implication, in giving
our account of the believer's side of the epistemological
division. The danger of proceeding in this way is that of
underestimating those elements in religious faith which cannot be reduced to cognitive terms. In turning to the discussion of the nature of faith we must do our best to
minimise this danger. I will first attempt to glean from our
preceding investigations those results that can give us a partial
account of what faith is. The man who has faith considers
himself to know that God exists and stands in certain relationships to the world and to men. In the terminology I have
introduced, the man who has faith considers himself to know
the truth of certain theistic statements. This supposed knowledge would enable him, if it is genuine, to prove other theistic statements, by combining this theistic knowledge with
other, non-theistic knowledge. The conclusions of these
supposed proofs would be of a sort that the sceptic, restricted as he is to non-theistic knowledge, must reject. It would
also enable him, if it is genuine, to verify other theistic statements by ascertaining the truth of some non-theistic statements, and combining this knowledge with the prior theistic
knowledge he considers himself to have. For in this combination this non-theistic knowledge might very well be adequate
to place some theistic statements beyond reasonable doubt.
The verification, once again, would be of a sort that the
sceptic, lacking prior theistic knowledge, would have to re-

112

ject. To say that he would reject such proofs or verifications is to say that he would have to deny that the theistic conclusions in question are thus proved or verified. The prior knowledge which the man who has faith considers himself to have has been obtained, if it is indeed knowledge, through revelation, not through proof. According to our analysis of the concept of revelation, this implies that the sceptic can accept the occurrence of the phenomena that the man of faith holds to be revelatory, but must reject that which is said to be revealed by them, and can do so without irrationality. This at least is so if there are no probative revelations, which we have agreed to be the case in accepting theological non-naturalism.

The above results, from our earlier discussions, suggest that the classical dichotomy that we find in St Thomas between faith and knowledge is mistaken. For if the man of faith really does know what he considers himself to know, his faith includes knowledge; and even if it does not, he thinks it does. But if this is so, we need to see why the classical dichotomy is so plausible. For we do not find it only in St Thomas; we find it in the popular picture of faith, current at least among unbelievers, in which faith consists of belief without adequate evidence, a more or less blind trust in obviously improbable propositions. To meet this need we have to examine the relation between faith and knowledge more closely than we have done hitherto. This is necessary for another reason. While I have accepted theological non-naturalism, I have denied that there is any necessary connection between its truth and the fact that most knowledge, or alleged knowledge, of God comes through revelation. I have questioned the view that the availability of proofs of God's existence, or of other theistic statements, would remove the need for revelation or the need for faith, and have attempted to undermine the traditional contrast between proof and revelation. This in turn suggests that the relation between faith and proof needs scrutiny also. I have already argued in Chapter 2 that even though a man may hold something on faith it could still be proved to him. We must also ask whether, if some truth is proved to him, he is thereby precluded from holding it on faith afterwards. Must that which one holds on faith be something which one has learned through alleged revelation, and not from proof?

We do not merely need to investigate further the relation between faith and knowledge, however. There is a great danger that in doing this we shall ignore the non-cognitive elements in religious faith, which are thought by many to be the most important. I rejected at the outset any suggestion that faith could be analysed in a way which described it exclusively in terms of these elements, but it is obviously impossible to ignore them. Not only is it not possible to ignore them, but their logical interrelationships with the cognitive element are such that neither can be understood without reference to the other. We have already seen how this interrelationship works in one direction. It is incoherent to say that someone trusts God without saying that he considers himself to know that God exists and is worthy of trust, which implies that the person who trusts God considers himself to know the truth of at least some theistic statements. Hence the non-cognitive elements of faith make no sense without a recognition of their dependence on the cognitive ones. It is easier to overlook the fact that there is a close dependence in the other way also. It can best be brought out by means of an example. Let us imagine a man who suffers some great personal calamity, such as the sudden death of his child. His faith in God enables him to endure this affliction, and sustains him through it. What is meant by such a statement? In part no doubt it means that because he is convinced of God's presence and God's love for him and his child he is able to feel sure that God's compassion and understanding are extended to him, as those of an understanding and compassionate human companion would be. In part no doubt it also means that because he is convinced of God's presence and love for him and his child he is able to be sure that the suffering and calamity will appear at last, under God's providence, not to be pointless and outside the divine will, but to be turned to a purpose which he may not now understand but in due course may. If either of these things is true, they show clearly enough how the trust that the man has cannot be understood without reference to the beliefs that he has. But let us look at the other side of this very complex situation. It is not just true that his faith sustains him in these ways; it is also true that his convictions are

114

sustained too. In sustaining him, his faith is being tested. Again, we may say here that instead of railing against God he submits to his will and trusts him; and once more we have something that makes sense only against a prior conviction of God's presence and goodness. But notoriously this is not all. For the very calamities that test his trust in God also serve to others as evidence against God's very existence. And this is a fact of which he will, as he faces these calamities, be very keenly aware. In so far as he does not himself come to doubt God's presence because of his experience, his faith is said to be strong; in so far as he does succumb to doubts, his faith weakens and is in danger of disappearing altogether. His belief in God is not something which he can abandon in the face of calamity in the way in which any tentative hypothesis can be abandoned in favour of another when the evidence seems to conflict. It is something to which he considers himself to be loyal or disloyal, faithful or unfaithful. The retention of his beliefs is, as it were, an achievement in itself, which the suffering he endures makes very difficult for him. Notice here that it is not, at least in this story, the fact of evil's existence that is his problem here, though men have abandoned belief in the face of this problem. His problem here is a personal one: although he has hitherto known that there are calamities, it is having to endure them himself that tests his faith. It is retaining his convictions about God in the face of experienced calamity and suffering that shows how much faith he has. Trust in God shows itself in the retention of convictions about him through calamity. We do not say that a man has faith if he agrees to all that is in the Creeds when untouched by calamity, and who does not care about it when it strikes him; we say this of the man who is stricken by it, understands and feels its full force, but retains his personal trust in God through it and retains his convictions about God also. To say that someone holds some proposition on faith, therefore, is in part to say that he holds on to it through adversity, that his holding it is an achievement, and a hard one. In this way we can see a relationship between faith and trust which works in the direction opposite from that which we observed before. Now we can see that the cognitive core of faith, or its persistence, is, in faith, a result of the trust that the man of faith has. The belief is not just the cause of the trust, but is also a manifestation of it. Any account of what faith is must be capable of incorporating this key fact. For it is this fact which makes believers and unbelievers judge faith so differently in moral terms: the former judging it as an achievement, and a fruit of grace, the latter as a paradigm of reprehensible obstinacy and failure to heed evidence.

Having stressed the importance of not confining ourselves to it, I will first return to the cognitive element in faith. I have so far said that the man of faith considers himself to know that some theistic statements are true. The matter cannot be left here. Does he consider himself to *know*? *Does* he know? Why not just say that he *believes*? Can one give a philosophically neutral account of the state of mind in which the man of faith finds himself?

In outlining Aquinas's account of the nature of faith, in which it is said to be an assent to propositions revealed by God, and to be due to divine grace, I noted that such an account seems to make it a necessary truth that one cannot have faith in false propositions. In the terminology that I have introduced in this work, this account of faith seems to result in the view that 'X has faith' is a theistic statement. It has been one of my objectives throughout to preserve philosophical neutrality regarding the truth or falsity of the statements about which believers and unbelievers disagree, and the statements I have made about the believer's state of mind have been intended as philosophically neutral in this way, and therefore not to be theistic statements. There is a clear conflict here which requires resolution. It might look as though this was easy enough. For the fact that some statement of the form 'X has $\emptyset$' is a theistic statement does not of itself prevent a philosopher from analysing the meaning of the concept represented by $\emptyset$ without committing himself to the existence of God. If one takes the statement that men are sinners, it is undoubtedly possible to give some philosophical analysis of what the word 'sinner' means without committing oneself to the theological scheme which is held to by those who use the term(1). Notice, however, what is involved in this way of preserving neutrality. To say that one can analyse the statement that men are sinners without committing oneself to any theology is to say by implication that one can describe what those who believe men are sinners mean by this

116

without committing oneself to the view that there are any sinners (since, of course, sin is alleged to be an offence against God, and one cannot admit that such offences occur without committing oneself to belief in God). So although theistic statements can be analysed with philosophical neutrality, this neutrality has sometimes to be purchased at the price of conceding that the correctness of the analysis is consistent with there being in fact no actual instances of the concepts used in them. This is one of the obvious differences between philosophical and theological analysis. To purchase neutrality in this way in the case of an analysis of the concept of faith would be to concede that there might not be any examples of faith. I have clearly not tried to proceed like this, but have taken it for granted that the state of mind I have been describing is one that some people are in. Is it, however, possible to give a philosophically neutral analysis of faith while holding that there are instances of it that the philosopher can identify? Clearly such an analysis will have to avoid commitment on the truth or falsity of what the man of faith holds; but can it? Can we assume that in saying a man holds certain things on faith we are not already conceding, of necessity, that some of what he holds is true? The account St Thomas gives requires that the truth of what he holds is by definition part of his faith, and would thus require this concession of us. Can we engage in the same debate without making it?

There is no neat way out of this difficulty. It is complicated by the fact that neutrality in a definition of faith might look like a cloak for a sceptical interpretation of it. Since to the sceptic belief in God looks like commitment on grossly inadequate evidence, and since scepticism is so common, the concept of faith has increasingly come to be used to refer to any state of mind in which someone, for commendable or at least forgivable motives, hangs on to some belief that he has no evidential right to hang on to. If he hangs on for motives that are thought to be reprehensible, he is likely to be said to be deceiving himself; though it may be called faith once again if he turns out to be correct after all. This use of the notion of faith seems to be derivative, the result of a certain kind of interpretation of the original article. The derivative notion is not of course restricted in its

117

application to religious beliefs. The danger of attempting to provide a philosophically neutral account of religious faith is that of appearing to interpret it as one instance of faith in this looser sense. Since the sceptic must, in rejecting the claims that the man of faith makes, hold also that his faith is belief without adequate evidence, believers are rightly suspicious lest philosophical neutrality be a cloak for a finally sceptical evaluation of their commitment. But it need not be. All that philosophical neutrality requires is that it is made clear, without a decision being made between them, where the man who has faith and the man who rejects what the man of faith holds, must offer opposed interpretations of the commitment the former has. I have already, in our partial accounts of faith, attempted to supply this. But this requirement returns us to the fact that such a two-pronged account presupposes that one can identify actual examples of the state of mind that is to be characterised in these competing ways; and on one reading of what faith is, even this presupposition looks tinged with scepticism.

I think it is possible to reach a limited accommodation with those theologians who consider that ascribing faith to someone entails accepting the truth of what he holds. It is, however, only a limited accommodation, and a reader must judge for himself how far the analysis of faith which I offer here is vitiated by inadequacies in it. If we look at St Thomas's account of faith, as I have attempted to summarise it in Chapter 1, we find that it contains, roughly, two kinds of proposition: propositions about the nature of the state of mind in which the man who has faith finds himself, and propositions about the origin of this state of mind and about the status of the doctrines to which he adheres. In the former class are the doctrines that faith is a form of assent to propositions, that it is wholehearted and voluntary, and that it is rational but not a form of knowledge. In the latter class are the doctrines that the assent of faith is due to divine grace, that the propositions held in faith are revealed by God, and of course that they are true. The obvious way to try to evaluate this account of what faith is while retaining a philosophical neutrality about the divine existence is to suggest that the former set of propositions are about faith itself, and the latter about its cause and its objects; to suggest,

118

in other words, that only the former propositions (or alternative propositions about the same state of mind) are properly about the concept of faith itself. If we cannot say this, then we cannot properly claim to be able to identify an instance of faith without accepting a theistic account of its origin and a theistic assessment of its content.

This is likely to be dismissed as much too simple. In a theological scheme in which faith is one of the supernatural virtues, and in which it is classified in order to have as its objects those true propositions which have been revealed by God, it is hardly acceptable to suggest that we could identify a case of it without knowing whether either of these theologically fundamental facts obtain. Furthermore, the connection between the concept of faith and the concept of *the* faith, which includes the notion of truth on its face, is likely to reinforce the opposition of those who adhere to the Thomistic tradition to any suggestion that there is no necessary connection between the existence of faith in a man and the truth of what he holds. The response I wish to make to this is the suggestion that the word 'faith' can be and is, used in two ways: the first way is as the name of an identifiable state of mind and personality; the second is as the name of that same identifiable state of mind and personality, plus the commitment that the state of mind is fastened upon true objects and has a divine origin. When it is used in the first way the ascription of faith to someone is not a theistic statement; but when it is used in the second way it is. It is of course not wrong to use it in either way rather than the other. For theological purposes it is no doubt most appropriate to use it in the second, theistic, way. In using it in this way to speak of someone's relationship to God, a theologian will be giving an additional interpretation to a phenomenon which can be recognised and referred to by someone who does not accept the claims about God that the man of faith makes. The analysis of faith that a philosopher can produce while maintaining religious neutrality is an analysis of the more restricted concept of faith, not the wider one.

But this still needs refinement. For what is characteristic about the state of mind referred to by the word 'faith', even in its more restricted and non-theistic use, is the very fact that the man who has it is himself committed to the very

E

119

kinds of propositions which those who use it in the more extended way wish to insist are part of its essence. The man of faith is certain to ascribe the existence of the faith he has to the grace of God; and he will certainly insist on the truth of the propositions he holds to! So it is very likely that an analysis, even the most philosophically neutral analysis, of faith will require us to say that the man who has faith is committed to the very propositions built into the concept of faith by those who insist that 'He has faith' is a theistic statement. This fact, however, is not damaging, though it restricts us in another direction. It prevents us from accepting any analysis, even a philosophically neutral analysis, that would allow the word 'faith' to be used univocally both of religious faith and of adherence to non-religious schemes such as Freudianism or Communism. There are analogies, often noticed, between the ways in which adherents to these secular schemes of thought sometimes cling to them and speak of them and the ways in which those who have religious faith behave and speak. Such analogies make it tempting to use the word 'faith' to speak of the states of mind of their adherents. This may be permissible, even illuminating; but we cannot admit that it then represents exactly the same concept if we are obliged to include the supposed objects of faith when analysing the objects of the state of mind referred to in religious contexts. In my terminology, the analysis of faith will not be expressed in theistic statements, but it will have to contain many theistic expressions. The partial characterisation of faith that I have so far offered as this argument has proceeded is, therefore, philosophically neutral in the way that this suggested accommodation requires, but this is not a way which enables us to apply the notion of faith we have been analysing to cases of these secular kinds (2).

I suggest, therefore, that the concept of faith that a philosopher can analyse differs from a specifically theological concept of faith in that the latter adds elements which cannot be included in the more restricted concept without committing one who uses it to the truth of the religious claims that the man of faith accepts. This position would enable the philosopher to offer his analysis to the theologian as a partial account of the concept that primarily concerns him. Such an accommodation is possible if the analysis of faith that the philosopher offers is one that includes as part of faith the adherence to specifically religious propositions, and if he does not attempt to produce a definition which is neutral in the further sense of fitting commitment to secular world-schemes or political movements.

If this accommodation is possible, it results in another possible accommodation: one with the religious sceptic. He can take over the analysis of faith that the philosopher offers and proceed to add to it claims about the causes or the effects of it which entail the *falsity* of the propositions to which the man of faith is committed - as, for example, Freudian theories of the nature of religious faith do(3). What the philosopher can do for both the apologist and the critic of religion is make clear what the nature of religious commitment is, so that some hope exists that their subsequent debate will be about the same thing.

I shall proceed as though this accommodation is possible. It depends, however, as the last paragraph makes clear, on agreement about a point of fundamental importance. I have assumed throughout that what is being analysed, religious faith, is a human phenomenon which is recognisable both by those who have it and by those who do not. I have assumed, that is, that the concept of faith is unlike that of revelation in that it is not only possible to give an account of what is meant by those who use it, but that it is possible with religious neutrality to claim that there are people who have it and that they can be identified. This might seem a mild enough assumption. It is, however, very easily questionable. If someone holds that faith is due to the grace of God, he does not need to deny, thus far, that someone who does not believe that God even exists can know that someone else has faith; for they may merely disagree as to what this shows, or what causes it. But if he insists that no state of mind can be called faith unless it is due to the grace of God, the position is different. Let us call our restricted sense of faith 'faith$_1$' and the inclusive, theological sense 'faith$_2$'. My suggested accommodation can then be expressed as follows: it is possible for someone who uses the word 'faith' to mean faith$_2$ to accept a philosophically neutral account of faith$_1$; this is possible because if there are any cases of faith$_2$ they are also, at least, cases of faith$_1$. That is, the disagreement is about the proper description of an agreed set of phenomena, for which two concepts, expressed with the same word, can be used. I do not think it is necessary to go so far as to insist that our accommodation requires in addition an agreement that all cases of faith$_1$ are also cases of faith$_2$ if faith$_2$ ever occurs(4); but it is necessary for the philosopher and the theologian to agree on at least some cases being cases of the phenomenon to be analysed, and even if this permits us to concede that there might be cases of faith$_1$ that were not cases of faith$_2$, the opposite concession is impossible. It is impossible because it would prevent our being certain that we could identify cases of each from an agreed list. A theologian, therefore, who rejected the thesis that all cases of faith$_2$ are cases of faith$_1$ would make it impossible for us to hold that the philosophically neutral account of faith$_1$ that the philosopher offers could be absorbed into his account of faith$_2$. He might be willing to pay this price, especially if he does not value philosophy much. He might be willing to pay it because he wishes to insist that only the eye of faith$_2$ can discern faith$_2$, or even that only God ultimately knows whether or not someone has faith$_2$, and he may feel that this insistence would be weakened if he agreed that an unbeliever could recognise the presence of necessary conditions for it. But the price he would pay would be higher than the mere abandonment of accord with philosophers. It would involve an abandonment of any hope that the unbeliever could come to any understanding, even a partial one, of what faith is, through a contemplation of the personalities of those that he is told have had faith. For it will merely be the authority of the believer that will assure him that these are cases of faith, and he will have no assurance whatever that any attitudes he finds common to the persons pointed out to him are necessary elements in the faith which they have had. He cannot be sure of learning anything of what faith is from studying the attitudes and personalities of St Paul, St Teresa, Isaiah or Luther. I do not wish to insist, in a non theological work, that such results are absurd ones. I merely state that the analysis of faith that concerns us is one which would only be theologically acceptable if the accommodation I have outlined can be made.

Part of the accommodation has been to include certain doctrines about the source of knowledge of God in the content of the propositions to which the man of faith is committed. This requires some expansion. It is, perhaps, possible for a very simple faith to exist without the person having it ever making explicit use of the notion of grace. If this is so, we could not say that the ascription of the alleged knowledge of God to divine grace formed part of the faith itself in all instances. What would have to be said would rather be that in this instance the faith consisted in a commitment to the truth of a body of doctrines, or to a tradition, which included such an ascription within it. This expansion has to be made to allow for the very numerous cases where unsophisticated believers, innocent of the theological agonies that have helped build up the traditions they inherit, have only a very partial understanding of what they believe.

Having achieved what philosophical neutrality is possible for us, let us return to our analysis of faith$_1$. I shall henceforth dispense with the numerical subscript.

(b) Knowledge and Faith

No neutral analysis of faith is possible unless considerable care is exercised about the use of the concept of knowledge. As soon as we say that the believer knows that p, we commit ourselves to the truth of p. I have so far made use of the statement that there are certain things which the believer 'considers himself to know', and that the sceptic denies that he knows them, because he denies that they are true, or can be known by anyone to be true. The sceptic, on this account, holds that the believer mistakenly believes these things. This account is neutral enough between the two to conform to our accommodation, and it permits the believer and the sceptic to make their incompatible claims without in so doing claiming anything that falsifies the philosophical account of them. But this is only a necessary condition of a sound philosophical analysis of faith, not a sufficient one. For it is only true if the believer himself would make use of the notion of knowledge in expressing the faith that he has, or would make use of notions that showed that he was committed to a claim to know. In particular, why the notion of

123

knowledge and not that of belief? In common with many others we have referred here to the man who has faith as the 'believer'. He himself is very likely at times (when he recites a creed, for example) to declare his faith to the world by saying that he believes certain things. A simpler sort of neutral account might seem to be readily available, which dispensed altogether with the notion of knowledge: it would merely state that the man of faith believed certain things; that the sceptic agrees that the man of faith believes them, and therefore agrees with the believer in the identification of the state of mind he has, but denies that the propositions he believes are true ones. Surely, in view of the nature of the epistemological deadlock that separates them, it is best to adopt this characterisation of their position? Does not the use of the notion of knowledge suggest what we have been at pains to deny, namely the existence of some agreed set of standards that will clinch the dispute in one direction?

The basic obstacle in the way of saying that the man of faith believes, rather than saying, more cumbersomely, that he considers himself to know, is the need to leave it undecided whether or not the man of faith does indeed know what he thinks he knows. It might be thought that saying he believes allows for his belief's being knowledge also. But to accept this is to accept by implication some analysis of the concept of knowledge that makes knowledge one species of belief - for example, justified true belief. Most philosophers would be inclined to accept such an account of it, and I do not wish to argue here that they are wrong to do so. But in dealing with the controversies in one philosophical area it is best to avoid unnecessary decisions on controversies in another. Saying that the man of faith considers himself to know certain things is compatible, if he *does* indeed know them, with his believing them, if it should turn out that an analysis of knowledge in terms of true belief is correct; if, on the other hand, it is not correct, the distinction between his state of mind and belief is already marked out by the use of this separate expression. I shall proceed, therefore, without assuming that the use of the word 'belief' to characterise his state of mind would guarantee the religious neutrality which I have been at pains to preserve, for to assume this would be to sacrifice neutrality in another very fundamental philosophical dispute. But the need to preserve neutrality in this latter controversy also forbids us to say that in the eyes of the sceptic the man of faith merely believes that which he considers himself to know; for that would suggest that the very use of the word 'believe' implies some element of doubt about the truth of that which is said to be believed; and however plausible this might be, it is a suggestion that tends to be emphasised by those who deny knowledge is a form of belief, and discounted or minimised by those who say that it is. So I say instead that the sceptic considers that the man of faith mistakenly believes. This is preferable, again, to saying that the sceptic holds that the man of faith mistakenly considers himself to know, for this locution carries within it an implied acceptance of the possibility that someone else can know these things, even though the person to whom this expression is applied does not; and most sceptics, if not all of them, either deny outright the truth of what the man of faith proclaims, or deny that anyone at all knows it.

The man of faith, then, considers himself to know certain things which the sceptic holds that he mistakenly believes. We have explored the nature of their disagreement sufficiently to add the following: apart from the special case of probative phenomena, which we have assumed to be absent *de facto,* their disagreement is not resolvable by the application of agreed standards. This does not mean that they do not each have standards: the sceptic insists on applying here exclusively standards that both sides would agree to apply in other spheres, and the man of faith has standards to which he will also submit disputes in which he is involved, as can be seen by examining the ways in which internal theological disputes are often settled among believers. It merely means that neither side will accept the sovereignty of the standards the other uses. It would seem to follow from this that each side can very well be in a position where it is proper to claim to know; in the believer's case, that certain theistic statements are true, and in the sceptic's case, that they are false or cannot be known to be true(5). Since they cannot both be right, only one of them can really know; but to say that each is entitled to claim to know is to say that the claim can, when the relevant standards are clearly satisfied, be invalidated only by the acceptance of the standards of the other side.

It is often thought that the task of epistemology is to understand the nature of knowledge in a way that enables us to say, *a priori*, when we have a case of knowledge and when not. With some subject-matters this aim can perhaps be realised. At least it is not part of my argument here to claim that it cannot be. But it is part of my argument that in the case of a religious subject-matter the aim is unrealisable. For the decisions that would need to be made in order to delineate a criterion for knowledge would already be theistic or atheistic decisions. If this is the task of epistemology, a religious epistemology is impossible.

There are two theoretical exceptions to this. First, an atheistic decision would be required of us if a fundamental incoherence could be found in theism. The failure of this line of criticism is something I have had to assume here, and not try to demonstrate. Second, a theistic decision would be required of us, as we have seen, if a sign were vouchsafed. But it does not seem to be. In both cases I say merely that the decision would be required of us. I have not said that anyone would do what was required.

Let us now return to our analysis of faith. I have defended the analysis of faith in terms of the man who has it being someone who considers himself to know certain things which the sceptic says he believes mistakenly, against the argument that it should be analysed in terms of beliefs. Two subsidiary questions must be faced now. Do those who have faith consider themselves to *know*? They themselves often proclaim that they *believe*. Surely only sophisticated and self-conscious believers consider that they know? What about the others?

Believers, of course, sometimes use the language of knowledge and sometimes that of belief when talking about themselves, and this does not make our task easier. It must be remembered that the language of faith has been forged in a world where those in the faith have been surrounded at all times by unbelievers, who have rejected the alleged revelations to which they have appealed, and it has been forged in part to speak to them. It must also be remembered that the doctrines that believers have proclaimed have been thought to be universal in their scope: their truth has been thought to be discernible in essentials by all men, however unsophisti-

126

cated, and revelation has been held to be available for all. It has therefore been a constant feature of Christian thought that Christians should say that they and their detractors have merely responded in opposite ways to the revelations that have been available to both. To say merely that the Christians know, and the pagans do not, would be to put the dispute on a level with that between a man who has musical sensitivity and a man who does not. Here the man who does can go his way feeling a mere disinterested regret for those of his fellows who cannot get anything out of Bach. But the man of faith is enjoined by his religion to convert his fellows. So even though, if the allegedly revelatory phenomena are revelatory, he does know that which is allegedly revealed by them, the omnipresent certainty of others' taking an opposite view of them makes it appropriate, throughout the ages, to use one epistemic term and its contradictory to express the acceptance and the rejection of what he proclaims. The same result is to be expected from the need of the Church in the early centuries to distinguish those who rightfully belonged to it from those, the heretics, who mistakenly believed things which they felt the Church should proclaim instead. The obvious way of expressing this difference is by singling out those things which the orthodox believe correctly from those which the unorthodox believe incorrectly; hence the language of the Creeds. It is too simple, in such circumstances, to argue that a language serving these functions is one which shows that its users did not consider that they knew that which they said that they believed.

Some may think that all this is on the side of those who think that knowledge is one kind of belief. Perhaps it is, and those who do not think knowledge is a sort of belief have to take account of it. But there are other facts, which those who think knowledge is a kind of belief have to take account of on the other side. I continue here to refrain from commitment on this wider epistemological issue. The point of the preceding paragraph is merely that of showing that even if knowledge and belief are exclusive, and their use to refer to one and the same state of mind implies differing judgements of it by the two speakers, the use of the concept of belief by Christians to speak of themselves has a ready explanation that does not entail that they do not consider themselves to know. If knowledge is a form of belief, the problem to which this is an attempted answer may not be a problem at all, but I am not assuming this to be so.

In Chapter 4 we examined the claim that the doctrines of the Christian faith are verifiable, and stressed that believers and sceptics would divide over alleged verifications in this life, but ought to agree that certain post-mortem experiences would be verificatory ones. I have not questioned Hick's claim that the eschatological elements of Christianity are essential to it, and I have tried to support this elsewhere(6). But it can remind us that these eschatological predictions normally include not only the deliberately restricted ones to which we confined ourselves, but other, more dramatic ones besides. In particular we have the claim that those who have shown faith in this life, if not others also, will be rewarded by a deeper understanding and vision of God. The life of faith here on earth is contrasted with the state of beatitude here-after, when faith, as the hymn has it, will vanish into sight:

> Beloved, now are we the sons of God, and it doth not yet appear what we shall be: but we know that, when he shall appear, we shall be like him; for we shall see him as he is (1 John 3:2).

> Now faith is the substance of things hoped for, the evidence of things not seen (Hebrews 11:1).

Faith, it appears, is something that we have need for in this life, and do not have need of hereafter. This is another reason for the great plausibility of the view that even to the man of faith himself, faith is not knowledge but something less, such as belief. But against this we must notice that the basic con-trast here is not between faith and knowledge, but between faith and understanding. That one can know only what one understands fully, and that such understanding is a form of intellectual vision (whatever that is) is a Greek doctrine deriving from Plato, and it is one which has seemed more congenial than it ought to seem to many Christian theo-logians. But aside from this, the fact that the faithful may expect to see God hereafter, though they do not now, and expect to understand his mysteries hereafter as they do not

128

understand them now, does not entail that they do not now know, or consider they know, the truth of what they proclaim. Even St Thomas, who holds that faith is not knowledge because the truths of faith are mysteries which human reason cannot fully understand, insists elsewhere that there are propositions which we can know to be true but which we cannot understand in more than a partial and fragmentary way, even though they are in themselves self-evident and capable of being understood; among these is the very truth that God exists. If one can prove, and therefore can know, the truth of propositions that one can only very partially understand, it seems inconsistent to hold that one cannot know revealed truths merely on the ground that these too are such that we cannot fully understand them. Of course if we could not understand them at all, even partially, then we could neither know them nor believe them. But if a dim understanding is allowed us, knowledge seems a theoretical possibility also. If our dim understanding gives place to a fuller understanding, no doubt our knowledge is immeasurably broadened and deepened; we now know better. But we still knew before. There are great difficulties about articulating the nature of the greater understanding that awaits the faithful, which is hardly surprising; this makes it important that we can give adequate content to eschatological predictions without having to lean upon it, but by relying only on the more limited understanding of theistic expressions which believers and unbelievers have at their disposal now. But for our present purpose it is enough to see that those who look for the vision of God do not thereby dismissss their present faith as something less than knowledge(7).

We have been looking at possible reasons for hesitating to say that the man of faith considers himself to know that which he has faith in. What, however, gives us positive grounds for using the word 'know' in such cases? The answer is, first and foremost, that there seems no other appropriate way of speaking of the mode of experience characteristic of the great formative figures of the Christian tradition. I quote Hick here:

To the Old Testatment prophets and the New Testament

apostles, for example, God was an experienced reality. He was known to them as a dynamic will interacting with their own wills; a sheer given reality, as inescapably to be reckoned with as destructive storm and life-giving sunshine, or the fixed contours of the land, or the hatred of their enemies and the friendship of their neighbours. The biblical writers were (sometimes, though doubtless not at all times) as vividly conscious of being in God's presence as they were of living in a material environment. Their pages resound and vibrate with the sense of God's presence, as a building might resound and vibrate from the tread of some great being walking through it(8).

The state of mind of these figures, as has been said so often, is analogous to that of someone who is in direct personal contact with another, greater, person. Such a one does not necessarily formulate a claim to know that he has converse with the other person; but we know that he would do so if his connection with that other person were challenged, or the very existence of that other person put in doubt. If it should turn out that the other person does not in fact exist, and that the one who thought he knew him has been the victim of illusion, it will still be true that he considered himself to know that he had dealings with the other. And to consider oneself to know this is to consider oneself to know at least some of the critical propositions about the other person that one could not fail to know if one indeed were in converse with him. In spite of the inappropriate contemplative overtones of the word 'consider', which I must explicitly discount, I prefer to use it rather than the word 'believe' in view of the reasons stated above. I would argue, therefore, that the recorded religious experience of the primary witnesses of the Judaeo-Christian tradition is such that it is only appropriate to use the language of knowledge to talk of it; since using the language of knowledge without qualification is obviously to presume the existence and presence of God, and since the occurrence of such experiences as those of the prophets and apostles can be known without knowledge of God, we need some phrase which will indicate that in the eyes of those having these experiences, they do indeed know of God, but that this does not show them right in this interpretation, or

130

show the sceptics who doubt it to be irrational in doing so. I offer for this purpose the statement that they consider themselves to know, emphasising that it is intended to cover, indeed in these instances primarily to cover, instances where there is no hesitation and no offering of reasons or grounds, but merely an instantaneous conviction - i.e. no process of consideration. The reason for preferring some locution involving the notion of knowledge is primarily the nature and tone of the documents which are supposed to record the experiences of the primary figures. Perhaps God exists, and perhaps not. Philosophy will not tell us. But *if* God exists, then Abraham and Isaiah and Peter and John and Paul *knew* that he does. And if he does not, they had everything that goes to make up knowledge except the truth of the proposition held to.

But these are figures of major religious stature. Most believers profess to no experiences of comparable depth or grandeur. Their commitment comes from an acceptance of the tenets of the tradition that hinges on the experience of the major formative figures, a tradition which they may enter by choice, or which they grow up in and remain. To such believers the tenets of the tradition are like the large and varied fund of common-sense knowledge that we inherit from our culture and never question. These latter are things that we would claim to know if we were challenged, and could often do no more than refer vaguely to some authority like our parents or schoolteachers to support if the challenge were pressed. Most of us have performed no tests to determine that the earth is round rather than flat, but claim to know it nevertheless. G. E. Moore centred many of his epistemological arguments on the fact that we would unhesitatingly claim to know such things even though we could not ourselves establish them. In a like manner innumerable believers have considered themselves to know the traditional tenets of their faith. Perhaps, if a common-sense proposition is challenged, we can offer adequate grounds for it, and perhaps not. If we cannot, then we did not know it; but we still considered that we did. If we can, then we do know it; then it is plausible to say that we did know it before; but even if we hesitate to say that, it is still true that we considered ourselves to know it before. In the case of religious propositions held from tradition, they may be abandoned when challenged; but believers still considered before this that they knew them. They may be defended by reference to allegedly revelatory phenomena, either within the experience of the believer facing the challenge or not; this appeal can be rationally rejected, but if the phenomena appealed to were revelatory, then he does know, and most likely did so before. And he certainly considered himself to know before.

We cannot as philosophers say that religious believers do know, or that they do not know, that which they consider themselves to know. But if God does exist and the phenomena they appeal to in support of their claims about him are indeed what they say that they are, there is no reason to say that their situation does not amount to knowledge. One could only properly deny this, *a priori,* if one could show that no knowledge-claim could be correct unless it was supported by the satisfaction of standards which all men, both those inclined to accept claims of this sort and those inclined to reject them, could accept. We have seen that the debate between believers and sceptics is not one that can be settled this way (failing probative phenomena). But this is not enough to show that believers' knowledge-claims are erroneous - only that they cannot be proved correct from non-theistic premisses(9)! We have already seen that the expectation of future experiences where faith gives place to understanding and where Christian claims are verified is consistent with the man of faith having knowledge now, which is enriched, deepened and vindicated then. As philosophers we can discern that they consider themselves to know; we cannot say that they are right so to consider, or that they are wrong. To say either is to adopt one of the competing sets of standards ourselves. But that is to step outside the philosopher's study. As people, we are often reminded, we have to do this. But to do it is to stop doing philosophy.

(c) Faith, Trust and Works

I shall now turn to the relation between the cognitive and non-cognitive elements in faith. It is primarily in terms of its non-cognitive elements that we have to understand the difference between faith and other forms of belief or alleged knowledge, and the difference between faith and the pig-headed adherence to prejudices. The best I can hope to achieve within the limited scope of this work is to indicate a rough outline of an account of what faith is, and how it can deal with these requirements.

It has often been pointed out that the adherence which the man of faith has to the doctrines that he proclaims is quite different from the adherence, if that is the word, which someone may have to some explanatory hypothesis, for example in the sciences. In the latter case some proposition is tentatively adopted, and our confidence in it is in proportion to the amount of confirmation it receives. If the evidence seems predominantly against it, it is abandoned. Religious belief is not tentative in this way, as indeed Aquinas says. This has been used to support the argument that religious beliefs are not subject to verification(10), but it is sufficient to recall our discussion of that notion to see the error of this argument. Even though the man of faith may think himself to know the tenets of his religion, and be in no way tentative about them, it does not follow from this that the claims he makes are not verifiable; and even though in the course of his experience in the faith he may encounter many verifications of what he holds and these may reinforce the faith which he has, this does not show the faith to be tentative rather than wholehearted. But while the adoption of religious doctrines is not different from the adoption of scientific hypotheses in lacking the potential for verification, it does indeed differ in being wholehearted, and in not depending on the subsequent verifications for the totality of the commitment involved in it. The basic reason for this total commitment is, as religious thinkers have always insisted, that faith is not only a state in which someone considers himself to know certain things about God, but is also a personal acceptance of and commitment to the God about whom these things are considered to be known. The distinction is often marked by the two Latin terms *fides,* for the acceptance of the propositions, and *fiducia,* for the personal commitment. The latter manifests itself in 'trust', which is the natural English translation of it (if we except the word 'faith' itself, which here comes to mean 'faith in' rather than 'faith that').

Because faith is *fiducia* as well as *fides,* the usual test of it is not the mere awareness that there are evils and trials and temptations, but the actual experience of them. Given that the man of faith considers himself to know that he is in God's hands and that God will care for him (and given also that the supposed divine promises to this effect are not, as most believers see the matter, spelled out in detail), the man of faith should have in his possession an antidote to anxiety. This is not the freedom from anxiety that we find in those who are unaware of the gravity of human crisis and suffering. There are superficial people like this, especially in a coddled society where suffering and death are hidden from sight or reduced to phenomena of entertainment. Indeed, their number seems on the increase. But there is no necessary connection between such attitudes and atheism. Not only may sceptics be free of it, but believers can exemplify it(11). Most of us are not unfamiliar with the very casual believer, whose life seems untouched by what he claims to know of God. Not only does he not seem to spend much effort in doing what his faith enjoins him to do, but he seems not to take seriously those very realities to which religious doctrines seem a characteristic human response. Such a person is 'of little faith'. In the Catholic tradition he is referred to as the *pococurante,* the man who cares little. Such a person seems to fulfil all our cognitive requirements for faith, but to lack, or show only very minimally, the trust which typifies faith in its full form. His kind of carelessness is not the fruit of faith but of immaturity.

It seems possible, then, to have the cognitive side of faith by itself, and when we find this we hesitate to say the person who has it has faith at all. The mere freedom from anxiety, even if associated with the supposed knowledge, does not seem enough. It has to be coupled with some degree of trust in the being about whom the subject considers himself to know. Perhaps we may feel some urge to say that someone who does not appreciate the gravity of life's crises does not really know, or does not have enough understanding to know, what it is he has accepted. Even if this urge persists, we can find other examples of those who have the cognitive but not the non-cognitive elements that go to make up faith. The classic example is that of the devils in St James:

134

Thou believest that there is one God; thou doest well: the devils also believe, and tremble (James 2:19).

Hick points out that the devils raise a problem for St Thomas's account of what faith is, since they seem to accept the very propositions that the faithful accept, and the acceptance of which St Thomas makes definitive of faith, and yet we do not want to say that they have faith(12). Thomas's solution is the unattractive one of saying that their acceptance is not meritorious, whereas the acceptance of the same propositions by others is; but this need not detain us. The example is one that best serves to lead us to the recognition of the existence of other possibilities, each representing various degrees of sinfulness in the eyes of the Christian tradition. One is the presence of the cognitive elements of faith combined not with trust but with despair, and a conviction, however irrational, that the divine grace is not available for oneself. Another, less dramatic and surely much more common, is the presence of the cognitive elements of faith combined with an unwillingness to give up those other, competing antidotes to anxiety, such as power or wealth, the enjoyment of which is not guaranteed to the man who trusts in God and has to be abandoned as a primary objective before such trust can be said really to exist. A third, rarer but discernible, is a combination of the cognitive elements of faith and an adoption, less or more consciously, of what in the Christian tradition are idolatrous practices and seem, even judged from outside it, to be perverse ones, such as Satanism and witchcraft. These cases, and others also, are enough to render intelligible the view that we can have belief without faith. Of course it is probably within the bounds of ingenuity to describe each of these cases in a way which entails that the subject, by his very lack of trust, does not really consider himself to know what he says he knows, but such descriptions are sure to be artificial. So far, then, although the non-cognitive elements in faith cannot in logic be present alone, the reverse is not true: belief without trust is indeed possible, and does not amount to faith when we find it.

The question of the relation of belief to faith, which we have been examining briefly, has to be distinguished from the traditional theological problem, over which much ink and blood has been spilled, of the relation between faith and works. Both the beliefs a man has, and the trust which he has, may show themselves in what he does. How close, however, is the connection? I cannot answer a question of this magnitude, but must make some brief comments. The answer has to be one that recognises that both trust and works are natural manifestations of the belief that men of faith have, and that works can be a manifestation of trust also, but that each concept must be kept distinct from the others. We all make the distinction between having a belief (or a piece of knowledge) and acting on it, yet we also use a man's actions and behaviour as indications of what his beliefs are. If we follow Socrates in insisting that it is a man's deeds and not his words that show what he believes (or knows), we notoriously lose the distinction between having the belief and acting on it, and construe all weakness of will as a sign of ignorance(13). The Christian doctrine of sin makes it quite impossible for those who accept it to adopt this consequence, which is in any case paradoxical to moral common sense; yet both Christianity and moral common sense make it mandatory for us to distinguish between what a man really believes and what he professes to believe, thus forcing us back to some degree on his actions and behaviour to determine what his beliefs are. It is enough for our purposes to say that the existence of a certain belief (or piece of knowledge) in a man is sufficient to lead us properly to expect certain appropriate actions and behaviour, so that if they are not forthcoming there has to be some reason for this. The obvious reasons, and the commonest, are laziness or fear or other forms of moral weakness, or prudence or some other deliberate restraint. There is, then, a logical connection between a man's having some belief and his acting or behaving in the ways appropriate to it, but this does not mean he *will* act on what he believes. In the case of religious beliefs, both a man's actions and his behaviour would be expected to include natural manifestations of the belief which he holds. In his actions, he would most obviously be expected to keep the commandments of the Christian faith. In his behaviour, he would naturally be expected to show a freedom from the anxieties and hostilities of which the trust in God is a cure. I have said that both trust and works are manifestations of

136

faith, and that works can manifest both the beliefs and the trust. It is now possible to outline this: (i) If a man considers himself to know the basic claims of the Christian religion to be true, this will manifest itself in his actions: he will tend to behave in love and charity towards his neighbours, and keep what he is taught to regard as the commandments of God. If he fails to do so, this will be because of weakness and sloth, and there will be some signs in his behaviour that he experiences some degree of guilt because of his failures, and craves forgiveness. If he considers himself to know these things, he will tend, without behaving carelessly or without reflection, to be free of anxiety about his future and will put his trust in God to care for him. But he may succeed or fail here also. It is one thing to know that God cares for you, and another to be freed by this from fear in the face of actual danger or disease or death. The man who fails to trust when the need arises may still perform good works, and may perform them because of his beliefs. But he may perform them as a kind of insurance, or from fear or duty rather than from trust. The knowledge he thinks he has may not issue in trust, but may still issue in deeds, which will then be done for the wrong reason. In such cases one would presumably have belief and works but not faith.

(ii) The man who has trust in God will do what he does in a spirit of trust: he will act out of love for the God he considers himself to know, not in order to stand in well with God and earn spiritual credit; he will not need to act from duty, even though what he does is that which it is man's duty to do; and although he will be fully aware of his shortcomings, his trust in the mercy of God will prevent his fearing the outcome of his deeds too greatly or of being hagridden by guilt when he fails.

(iii) This all seems to suggest that it is logically impossible to show trust in God without doing the works enjoined in the Christian tradition. But there are exceptions here too. If one has trust then what one does will be done in a certain manner. But without some determination and effort to follow these commandments, one may yield to forms of socially irresponsible resignation, where one is so confident of God's care that one does not bother to do what he is said to enjoin to help those in need, and where one is so confident

137

of forgiveness that one does not bestir oneself to exert more than a token effort; and here one has the dead faith, that does not issue in works as it should.

The upshot seems to be that faith and works are distinct; that one naturally but not necessarily leads to the other; that faith necessarily involves both supposed knowledge and trust in the God of whom one supposes oneself to know; that the trust cannot in logic exist without the supposed knowledge, but that the supposed knowledge can exist without the trust; and that where it does we do not have faith, though we may indeed have works.

I now wish to return to the case of the man who has his faith tested by tribulations. He may, prior to this, have considered himself to know enough about God to be able to make any necessary intellectual accommodations to the facts of evil and suffering in the world. But it is only when they affect him, or those dear to him, or those about whom he can care deeply, that it can be tested what manner of faith he has; for only in the face of experienced tribulation can it be seen how deeply he trusts in the God of whom he considered himself heretofore to know. His trust will perhaps sustain him through the tribulations, but in its turn it will be tested by them. There are, to be crudely schematic, two major types of risk to which his faith is exposed. The first involves his trust, and the second the supposed knowledge on which it depends. (i) His trust is shown to be weaker than it should be if he is unable to avoid inconsolable grief, or hopelessness, or, in particular, resentment and hatred. If each of these takes hold of him, then his faith has been inadequate. He has failed to be comforted by God's love, and to be reassured by God's promises. But these failures of faith can take place, and often do take place, without the person guilty of them ceasing to consider himself to know that God exists, and that God has made these promises. He may merely, through human weakness and (as Christianity sees the matter) through sin, fail to sustain the trust which is the natural expression of such knowledge. He may show the conflict this engenders in many ways: he may pray to the God whom he does not trust as he ought, for power to trust him more; or he may rail against the God whose providence he really knows better than to resent, or whose promises he really knows better than to

138

doubt. There may be some element of irrationality in such conflicts but this hardly shows they cannot occur. Nor does their occurrence show that the cognitive state of the man who thus fails (or, for that matter, the cognitive state of his fellow-believer who succeeds) is not one of knowledge. For we can either succeed or fail to guide our conduct or govern our attitudes by the knowledge that we have. So a common state where faith is being tested is one where a man will show a greater or less degree of trust toward the God of whom he considers himself to know.

(ii) A more complex situation arises when the very conviction of God is itself threatened. The distinction between the former case and this one is not a sharp one, especially in a developed theism. It is not easy to be sure when failure to trust the being whom one considers oneself to know is nevertheless worthy of trust gives place to doubt whether he is thus worthy after all, although the distinction between the two is clear. In a developed theism, moreover, no exact line can be drawn between doubting whether God is worthy of trust and doubting whether he even exists. Let us take the most famous instance in the literature of someone whose trust in God is shaken: the case of Job. Job, at least on one obvious interpretation, curses the day on which he was born and rails against Yahweh because of the calamities that have afflicted him. But he never doubts that Yahweh exists: indeed he could hardly do this while railing at him. But in the Book of Job we do not have an instance of fully-developed theism as we find this in Christianity. This is not because it is a Jewish and not a Christian document, but because it is one of the documents illustrating the development of the Christian idea of God. The Christian idea of God is one which has goodness built into it. In consequence of this, we do not now show interest in doctrines of finite deities, who are good but not all-powerful, or all-powerful but not all-good. Any being worthy of the title of 'God' must be considered to be both. In our parlance, Job is railing against Yahweh because he doubts, in the light of his calamities, whether Yahweh is really God; whether, that is, he is worthy of the service he has rendered him and the trust he has placed in him. But he can wonder about this without wondering whether Yahweh exists. A Christian cannot consistently wonder whether God

139

is worthy of trust, whether he has the qualities that make it rational to trust him, without doubting his very existence. This is a necessary feature of any developed theism which accords perfect goodness to the deity. A Christian who allows his calamities to affect not only his trust in God but his conviction of God is passing from a state in which he feels his trust failing him when he thinks he still knows very well that he ought to manifest it because of what he knows of God, to a state where he does not have it and begins to consider that he is perhaps right not to; but this can only mean that perhaps God does not exist after all, that the sky at which he shakes his fist is empty.

There is always the danger that our first case will give way to our second, and that faithlessness will lead to apostasy. This is because of the human being's constant thirst for rationality, which is not always beneficent in its results. It can lead to our creating beliefs to match our attitudes (which is what sceptics say believers do) and to our destroying beliefs when our attitudes change (which is what happens when faith is lost and belief abandoned). This is why the retention of the alleged knowledge of God can appear to men of faith as an achievement. When trust is shaken and this gives place to doubt, this is likely to be in the face of the experience of the very phenomena which sceptics point to as reasons for not accepting Christian claims about God in the first place. Where these phenomena do not produce a lessening of trust, it is clear that the very trust the man of faith has, by pre-empting his anxiety about these phenomena, prevent his intellectual accommodations of them from being undermined - hence his appearance of pig-headedness to the sceptic. Where trust is shaken, but conviction is not, the concern this engenders for the believer is of a quite different order from the concern which the sceptic feels he ought to have - hence what to the sceptic is a combination of obstinacy, wishful thinking, and misplaced guilt towards a non-existent object is to the believer a struggle to live up to the implications of what he knows. Where the lessening of trust leads to a weakening of conviction, the resulting state of mind will be one of considerable complexity. In so far as there is some trust and conviction remaining, the weakening of the conviction in the existence of God will be bound to

140

seem the worst sort of personal betrayal and lack of trust in God, and to generate a guilt which is virtually incomprehensible to the sceptic, for whom the question of the adoption or abandonment of beliefs carries with it no issue of loyalty to anything except the evidence. Since the degree of loss of trust has to be considerable before it can lead to loss of assumed knowledge, and since prior to its doing so the very extent of it will be a cause of shame and remorse, the loss of the conviction of God will carry the same load on its first appearance, and only shed it when the conviction has finally gone, if it goes even then. If it begins to be shaken, but is then reinstated, this is bound to appear, and perhaps to be, a moral achievement and a sign of renewed trust in God on the part of the believer.

Once again we must insist that none of this shows that what is lost, or regained, or threatened or sustained, is not knowledge. For we can succeed or fail in showing in our attitudes the appropriate effects of the knowledge that we have. If we fail, we may very well seek to justify this by putting in question the very things we considered that we knew; things which, if true, show our attitudes to be reprehensible. So a breakdown of faith which leads to total apostasy may indeed be a case of a man's losing, through lack of steadfastness, knowledge which he previously had. This could be true even if the knowledge was based on proof. For we can cease to know that which was once proved to us. So even a world where men had all they needed to know of God proved to them, and then knew it, would be a world in which they needed faith; for adversity can destroy knowledge, however that knowledge is acquired.

The assumed knowledge that the man of faith has does not only have to sustain itself in the face of adversity, or in the face of phenomena which appear as counter-evidence. These certainly are enough to account for the complexities of faith, which the believer and the unbeliever interpret so differently: granted the believer's supposed knowledge of God and his consequent reliance on God's promises, his trust is well founded, though those who lack this supposed knowledge must regard his trust as no more than ill-advised adherence to dogma in the teeth of counter-evidence. But the believer is surrounded by such sceptics; so were the early Christians. It is therefore not surprising that the sceptics' evaluation of the nature of faith has come to form part of the common understanding of the term. There is another and more serious consequence of the fact that faith exists amidst scepticism. This is the acceptance on the part of believers themselves of the sceptics' contention that adherence to religious claims cannot, however we regard it morally, be a form of knowledge. Given the limitations of what he can claim to know, the sceptic must make this judgement, but there is no good reason why the man of faith himself should agree to it. For faith is needed even if the propositions held to in faith are known. For men can lose their knowledge, and men can fail to live up to it, and men can fail to be as free from anxiety and resentment and fear as their knowledge should make them. The antithesis of faith and knowledge, once conceded, requires a further concession on the part of apologists that they should not make: that knowledge of the truth of theistic statements is something that could only come if they were proved from non-theistic ones - that is, if they were established by an epistemic procedure that could be accepted as genuine by both sides. But nothing of importance to faith is preserved by this concession, and much is lost. Much is lost because it follows from it that only if they had access to such proofs could the greatest figures of the religious tradition be said, even by their followers, to *know* that God exists. Nothing is gained because, even if (though we have denied this) such proof from non-theistic premisses were possible, it need not lead to knowledge or add to the number of believers. Faith would still be needed in the face of adversity and unbelief, neither of which need be lessened in extent by the existence of proofs. For faith to be needed, theological non-naturalism does not have to be true. For faith to be needed there does have to be evil to contend with, and there do have to be those who deny that God exists. In the face of these obstacles, faith faces all the tests that we know it to face. They are obstacles it would have to face even if the knowledge that is part of it could be established through proofs; for these would not remove the evils, nor necessarily lessen the denials.

For faith to be requisite we do not need a world in which it is not clear that God exists, even though that is the world

142

that we have. We merely need a world in which many men behave as though he does not exist. To say that they would not behave in this way even if it were clear that he does, or even if it has been proved to them that he does, is to pay a quite unwarranted tribute to human rationality and willingness to face realities: a tribute which the Christian tradition has never countenanced. It is of course quite rational for them to behave as though he does not, when they find themselves in a world where it is not clear that he does. And again this prompts the question: what theological reason could there be for the existence of such a ready justification of their behaving in this manner, if he does?

I turn in conclusion to some brief comments on the two accounts of the nature of faith that I outlined in Chapter 1.

(d) Two Accounts of Faith

Aquinas tries to establish the credentials of revelation by means of proof. Our account suggests that there is nothing amiss with this in principle, but that in practice the attempt fails because the proofs fail. Hick criticises Aquinas for holding on the one hand that the credentials of revelation can be established, and on the other that in accepting revelation in faith a man is a free agent. There is indeed an inconsistency here, and it comes from St Thomas's belief, which Hick shares, that there is a necessary connection between the voluntariness of faith and the alleged fact that its propositions cannot be proved. If there is such a connection, then the closer St Thomas comes to the view that revealed truths can be proved, the closer he comes to having to abandon the voluntariness of faith, which he cannot abandon. But we have seen that there is no necessary connection. Since there is not, we can say that whether one has faith or not is independent of whether the propositions of faith are revealed or proved. Indeed there is no reason in logic why they should not be both.

Faith and knowledge, then, are not exclusive. The voluntariness of faith is not inconsistent with a man's knowing its propositions to be true, since he could have refused to accept them, either from proof had such existed or from revelation. Nor is the fact that its propositions tell of mysteries that are

143

beyond human understanding inconsistent with their being known to be true, even though the knowledge that men could have of such matters would be shallow and incomplete compared with that promised to them hereafter.

St Thomas may or may not be wrong in insisting that revelatory phenomena are themselves propositions. But even if they are not, they cannot be accepted as revelatory without propositional commitment on the part of the person accepting them. The fact that revealed propositions can be rejected does not, however, show that they cannot be proved as well as revealed, or that they cannot be known to be true. Furthermore, the fact that faith entails supposed knowledge of propositions does not make such supposed knowledge enough for faith.

Aquinas wishes to show that faith is rational by basing it on philosophical knowledge of God; but to show it to be voluntary by denying it is itself a form of knowledge. It could, however, be both voluntary and a form of knowledge; and what prevents it being rational in the way he wishes is the *de facto* absence of proofs of theistic conclusions based on non-theistic premises. It still can contain proofs and verifications of the kind the sceptic must reject, however, so it is rational after its own fashion. We still await a good theological reason why it should not also be rational after his.

John Hick rejects the dichotomy of faith and knowledge, but still argues that the knowledge the man of faith considers himself to have cannot be of the sort that a proof from non-theistic premises could provide, since this would detract from men's freedom to reject God. I have agreed that faith could be a form of knowledge, or rather include a form of knowledge, and also that its claims are in principle verifiable. But I would argue that the compatibility of faith and knowledge could extend equally to propositions that had been proved from non-theistic premises, since men could still, even if such proofs existed, refuse to accept them, and the knowledge that they had if they did accept them would still need to be maintained through faith. Human freedom could still coexist with successful proofs of God: and one can still wonder why it does not do so.

Hick's account of faith, which treats the formative events of the tradition as the revelatory phenomena and the propo-

144

sitions to which men adhere in faith as interpretations of them, allows for proper weight to be given to the non-cognitive element of faith, the supposed personal response to God, and allows for some degree of doctrinal differences in the face of one and the same revelation. It does not, however, in practice or in intent, remove the essential core of know-ledge-claims from the believer's avowals of faith. He still must consider himself to know that God exists, and to know some critical truths about him, even if the proclamation of these is the expression of his interpretation of the revelatory phenomena, rather than a revelatory phenomenon itself. So our discussion of the relation of knowledge to faith is as appropriate a discussion of his account of faith as it is of that of St Thomas.

I have not hitherto commented upon Hick's suggestion that faith, being an interpretation of phenomena that the sceptic refuses to interpret in the same way, can be construed by analogy with the perceptual phenomenon of 'seeing-as'. Wittgenstein draws our attention in the 'Investigations' to the way in which certain ambiguous pictures can be seen in more than one way - as a duck at one moment, and as a rabbit the next, for example. Hick attempts to extend this description of some perceptual situations along lines reminiscent of post-Kantian idealist theories of perception, to cover all seeing, and to illuminate the nature of religious faith(14). These accounts of perception stress the extent to which elements of inter-pretation enter into our day-to-day awareness of the world around us, where we constantly (or so these theories have it) invest our perceptual data with meaning. It is a matter of much controversy how far we could refrain from doing this, or from doing it in a particular way. Could we succeed in an attempt *not* to experience our percepts *as* manifestations of physical objects in a law-abiding world? Or *as* anything what-ever, other than passing sensations? The duck-rabbit analogy, if pressed, suggests that any particular interpretation, how-ever fundamental to our thinking, could be switched on and off again at will, and even perhaps that we could manage without adopting one at all. But how good an analogy is it? What concerns us here is not the value of the analogy as a way of understanding perception, but its value as an aid in understanding the specifically religious interpretation of experience characteristic of faith. In many respects it is a happy analogy, and our discussion confirms that it is: both faith and scepticism can incorporate rational and self-consistent world-views, and one and the same phenomenon can be read in terms of one world-view or the other. But what about the ability to switch such a world-view on and off? Can one do this, in particular, with the Christian world-view? Even though the adoption of 'the alleged knowledge that faith contains is unforced in the manner that we have seen, its voluntariness does not extend this far. For in faith one holds to the Christian interpretation of things. Anyone who could switch it on and off, as we can switch on the rabbit-reading and then off again, would show he did not have faith after all. This does not mean that men cannot switch the Christian world-view on and off; it merely shows that those who can do so do not have faith. A sceptic can do it: when reading Dostoevsky or Graham Greene or the Psalms, he can, for a while, switch on the Christian view of the world that is expressed in these works. This is an imaginative exercise, which he can perform at will, to be broad-minded, to see things as his opposite number within the faith sees them. He can of course do this without for a moment believing the world really to be as he is willing for a little while to see it. His suspension of disbelief does not go deep, for he never ceases to think Christianity is false. The believer can perform the same imaginative exercise in reverse, remaining a believer all the time he does it. To define faith as seeing-as, though suggestive, carries the misleading suggestion that the man of faith sees the world as the Christian tradition interprets it, in this imaginative or aesthetic fashion; but of course only someone who does *not* have faith can adopt the Christian view in *this* way. The believer *believes* it.

(e) Conclusion

I have tried to offer some account of the epistemic status of religious faith as it confronts an increasingly widespread scepticism. This has required examination of the apparent truism that God's existence cannot be proved, and of the controversy generated by the insistence of some sceptics that religious claims are unverifiable. It has also required

146

examination of the status of the claim that knowledge of God comes through revelation, and of the interaction between the allegedly cognitive element in religious faith and the non-cognitive elements in it. There is no need here to recapitulate all the conclusions of our arguments, but one or two general morals seem to be in order as we conclude.

While we are often too confident in proclaiming it, it does seem to be true that the world we live in is not one that will provide adequate raw material for a proof of God's existence, or of any theistic statement, from non-theistic premisses. Traditional natural theology, which set out to provide such proofs and to demonstrate the irrationality of scepticism, seems a hopeless undertaking. Yet for all this shows us, God may still exist. But even if he does, it is not irrational for those who do not believe this to retain their disbelief. But again, even though this is true, others may, if he exists, still know that he does, because truths about him have been revealed to them. Some have argued that this epistemic division is just what we should expect if God does exist and has the character that is ascribed to him in the Christian tradition. For he would not force recognition of himself upon his creatures. Now the fact that something is what we would expect if some belief were true does nothing to show it *is* true. It only shows that it might be true; so the sceptic can still maintain with the fullest reasonableness that it is not true, or that no one knows that it is. But once again, it might be said, the ambiguous situation we find is the most that can be expected. If there were more than this, men would have to acknowledge that God exists, and their cognitive freedom would be undermined. For it would then be irrational for them not to acknowledge God.

It is my major contention that this is a bad argument. It would only hold good if men's cognitive freedom were such as to prevent them from being irrational, and stop them from denying what it is unreasonable to deny. But we need no *a priori* arguments, and no further analysis of the concept of cognitive freedom, to see that this is not so. For men often disbelieve things that are beyond rational doubt.

I do not suggest that the absence of proofs is something the believer cannot accommodate; and it certainly does not prove scepticism to be true. For this, a disproof of God's existence would be needed, and we do not have this either. I suggest something much less fundamental, but of more than academic interest nevertheless: that even though men of faith should not be daunted by the absence of proofs, they should not be so eager to welcome it that they disregard the work of those religious thinkers who try to provide them, or assume that it must misrepresent what Christian claims are. Natural theologians may have failed, but it is misguided of their fellow believers to say this serves them right. We have seen some of the consequences of deciding that theological non-naturalism is true. The problem of why it is true if God exists may be a minor problem to an apologist, but it is hardly a trivial one. Perhaps, after all, they should not accept theological non-naturalism but challenge it. Both believers and sceptics should take very seriously the fact that it rests on foundations that can still be debated.

Appendices

The following comments deal with topics on which I have touched briefly in the text, but which it would have been disruptive of the main argument to include within it. I do not think that the main argument depends on what I say about these issues, but it would have been unwise to ignore them altogether.

Appendix A: Self-deception

The concept of self-deception has drawn a fair amount of attention from philosophers recently, and it is clearly a difficult notion to analyse coherently. It has not been my purpose to offer any analysis of it in the text, but merely to insist that it is a concept which has application, and that it is one of the ways in which men who have had something proved to them may turn away from it. Self-deception has to be distinguished from other states of mind which shade into it and can easily be confused with it. I have stressed particularly that it is different from ignorance or hypocrisy, even though it is easy to be doctrinaire and insist that any given case of it is really a case of one of these.

In an essay published in 1964 I attempted a brief outline of the necessary and sufficient conditions of self-deception (7). I will first restate the position, and then comment on some recent criticisms of it. The concept of self-deception has seemed to some to generate paradoxes, to make us claim, for example, that a man both does and does not believe the same proposition - for he must believe it if he is to deceive anyone, himself included, that it is false when it is true, yet he must also disbelieve it if he is to be deceived that it is false when it is true. It has been argued that such difficulties come from trying to understand the idea of deceiving oneself on the model of that of deceiving others. If we resist this temptation, a non-paradoxical rendering seems less difficult. Gustavson and Canfield, who draw our attention to the dangers of using the model of other-deception, try to avoid

149

these by arguing that self-deception is merely belief in the face of strong evidence (2); but this is not enough. Certainly it is a necessary condition, for if the subject's belief were not held in the face of strong evidence, self-deception would be indistinguishable from intellectual indecision, or caution, or inertia. But the self-deceiver must also know the evidence; or else we have not self-deception but ignorance. Further, if he knows the evidence yet does not accept what it points to, this might be because he does not *see* what it points to, and then we have stupidity or naïveté; so the subject must not only know the strong evidence, but see what it points to. But if he has, knows and sees the import of strong evidence, what is left for him to do to believe what it points to? It is not at all clear what is added by the notion of acceptance in such a context; for the criteria for saying that he really does see where the evidence points and the criteria for saying that he accepts the conclusion to which it points are the same. In this case, what are we saying when we insist that a man in this position may *not* accept that which the evidence he knows points to?

The only way of avoiding the reinstatement of a paradox here is to accept the fact which paradoxical renderings feed upon: that self-deception is a conflict-state. This way we can settle for consistent description of inconsistent behaviour. Someone in this state does partially satisfy the criteria for belief and also those for disbelief - in particular he will tend to declare his disbelief in that to which he sees the evidence points. If he is deceiving himself that something is so when the evidence is in favour of it (a condition we may call self-simulation) he will tend to declare it to be so. If he is deceiving himself that something is not so when the evidence is in favour of it (a condition we may call self-dissimulation) he will tend to declare it not to be so. Now I have already suggested that the criteria for his really seeing where the evidence points and those for his accepting the conclusion to which it points are the same. To this we must add the complementary point that there must be some reason to hold that the self-deceiver does not believe what he asserts (or there would be nothing for him to deceive himself over), and yet there must be some reason to say that he does believe what he asserts (or there would be no deception towards himself, merely lying towards us).

In view of these considerations, I suggested that the severally necessary and jointly sufficient criteria for self-deception over matters other than one's own inner states are (i) belief in the face of strong evidence, (ii) the subject's knowledge of the evidence, (iii) the subject's recognition of the import of the evidence. These add up to a conflict-state in which there is partial satisfaction of the opposed criteria for belief and for disbelief, with the subject's declarations likely to be against the evidence.

Fingarette (3) has criticised this outline on two major counts. One is that the last sentence characterises the conflict-state in terms of partial satisfaction of the criteria for belief and disbelief, whereas item (i) in the list of criteria for self-deception merely reads 'belief'. The other is that if it is true that the criteria for someone's seeing the import of the evidence, and for his accepting that which it points to, are indeed the same, the items (ii) and (iii) add up to belief in the truth of the conclusion to which the evidence points; this then makes my characterisation of self-deception equivalent to the subject's holding two incompatible beliefs, and reinstates the paradox it was partly designed to avoid. These criticisms are fair enough, given the wording of the original account. To avoid them I suggest the following: what is, first of all, unhappily suggested by the use of the word 'partial' is the fact that in a case of self-deception we have signs which, in the absence of contrary signs, would add up to the satisfaction of criteria for belief, and also, unfortunately, signs which in the absence of contrary ones, would add up to satisfaction of the criteria for disbelief. There is too much to go on rather than too little, and the upshot of it (and here my formal criteria are indeed misleading) is that it is not clear that he believes or that he disbelieves. If he stopped showing signs of disbelief also, his belief would be obvious, and vice versa; but because this does not obtain, we are unclear. We are unclear because *it* is unclear. I do not know any better way of characterising the conflict-state than this, and will not attempt another formal list because I do not presently see how to do so. One result of these modifications is to force qualification in the statement that the criteria for someone's seeing where the evidence points and the criteria for his accepting the conclusion to which it points are the same. While the same behaviour is indeed sufficient for both in most cases, this is one of the things that is obscured in cases of self-deception. For here it is quite likely that the way in which he shows what belief he has in the proposition he proclaims against the evidence, and the devices (such as the one mentioned from J. F. Ross in Chapter 2) which he resorts to in order to reinforce his protestations, are the key signs that he does indeed see where the evidence is really pointing. Where the way he supports the belief he proclaims evinces his uneasiness in the face of the contrary evidence, it is plausible to argue that the same behaviour manifests both whatever belief he has in one proposition and his awareness of the fact that the evidence before him points to its contradictory. I do not think this is paradoxical, but it is indeed more complex than my formula allows.

Fingarette argues further that the threefold formula does not distinguish self-deception from indecision. If someone satisfied my three conditions, specially as qualified, might we not say that he was just dithering between two views, uncertain which to accept? We might indeed, and he might say so himself. The man who deceives himself will not say so. For intellectual indecision is not destroyed by being proclaimed, whereas self-deception clearly is. The self-deceiver is someone who is not ready to *acknowledge*, even though his behaviour and his actions will tend to *show*, his recognition of the import of the evidence in the face of which he proclaims the contrary proposition. The addition of this element is necessary to distinguish self-deception from other kinds of case which are cited by Gardiner (4): 'half-belief', hunches, and unshakeable belief in a lucky star, all of which can be explicit. It is the addition of this element which, if I understand him correctly, Gardiner himself thinks will make an analysis on the lines I first suggested seem plausible.

When it is added, it becomes important to consider with care the place of motive in self-deception. It is not included in my original formula, simply because I considered the motive for which something is done not to be a proper part of an analysis of *what* is done. Self-deception, however, is thought of as an action and held to be reprehensible because

152

even though not consisting of actions alone, it contains essentially deliberate or intentional elements like the unwillingness to acknowledge what one sees or the determined, even aggressive, insistence on that which the evidence does not support. It is the presence of these intentional elements, which Fingarette makes central to his analysis of self-deception, that makes Gardiner right to hesitate over the very attractive and simple suggestion that self-deception might be just error-with-a-motive, and ordinary error be error-without-a-motive. For error is necessarily not deliberate. Freudian accounts of errors, that ascribe unconscious motives to them, turn them into deliberate actions at the deeper level. In self-deception the deliberate elements can be discerned, and therefore the distinction between it and error has to be maintained in a form that does not relegate them to the unconscious.

Gardiner offers the fact of wishful thinking as an objection to an analysis of self-deception as error-with-a-motive. The difference between these is in fact partly explicable by motive. For self-deception is typically motivated by fear or guilt, whereas wishful thinking is motivated by desire or hope. But the crucial difference lies somewhere else. Self-deception involves showing all the signs of believing something, and proclaiming it, when the evidence is against it. It is a reaction against, an opposition to, the evidence. Wishful thinking can occur when there is no evidence against the proposition believed at all: it is a too-ready acceptance of a proposition when the evidence is inadequate. As Descartes saw, it is a weak-willed refusal to suspend judgement, and a leap beyond what evidence there is in the direction that it faintly points. If self-deception is a conflict-state that is reprehensible, wishful thinking is reprehensible because there is no conflict when there ought to be.

Finally, what is the exact nature of the contrast between self-deception and faith? In my original essay, I made the following comment: that when someone who has held to some proposition in the face of evidence that is strongly against it, turns out nevertheless to have been right, we do not say that he has been deceiving himself, but that he has had faith. Gardiner takes the example of Hitler's belief in his destiny, which he held to in the face of the most overwhelming counter-evidence, as a case of faith, and says correctly, as we have seen, that in such a case the subject's state is not one which would be destroyed by being made fully self-conscious, any more than intellectual indecision need be. He also points out that in such a case we are able to take it for granted that Hitler's state of mind involved adherence to false propositions, not true ones. My original comment was not intended to define the nature of faith, but only to indicate one of the circumstances in which the accusation of self-deception might be retracted in favour of a more complimentary description. It still seems to me that if we had a person who held to a proposition in the face of strong contrary evidence, and did this in the manner which would normally be taken to amount to self-deception (with an unacknowledged but real awareness of what the evidence pointed to, and the rest), but then turned out to be right in what he had overtly maintained, the word 'faith' would then be the natural one to use. Indeed this does not provide us with much to go on if we are trying to say what faith is, and I was not attempting to make the distinction between self-deception and faith hinge upon this.

In this context it is noticeable that calling the subject's state self-deception entails an unfavourable evaluation both of the epistemic status of the proposition he proclaims, and of his adherence to it; whereas changing the name to faith at least softens the evaluation, even though the truth of the proposition is something he was in no position to know while he held to it. The non-religious use of the word 'faith', which I have not tried to analyse at all fully in this book, usually carries with it this overtone of acceptance, if not approval. Non-religious faith is, very roughly, the morally understandable, or even morally good, adherence to a proposition when the evidence is weak, or even strongly against it. When the evidence is weak, but not adverse, a hostile critic will accuse the subject of wishful thinking. When the evidence is adverse, he will tend to accuse the subject of pig-headedness or obstinacy: even the passage quoted by Gardiner is respectful when speaking of Hitler's 'faith'. When the evidence is adverse and the subject displays the symptoms of recognising this but does not admit to it, it is self-deception of which his critics will accuse him. When he turns out to be

154

right, the disapproval tends to vanish (as it does when we find the thief is Robin Hood) and the word 'faith' is the natural one. Religious faith, which I have tried to analyse at some length, is a state which I have suggested is not only called for when the evidence is weak or adverse, but also needed when the subject thinks it to be conclusive. The fact of the believer's adverse environment, or the impact of personal suffering upon him, may put it to such tests that his belief may depend upon his trust in God. Viewed from outside, as the sceptic sees it, this too is just adherence to propositions which the evidence either does not establish, or is strongly against. So in times of calm the man of faith looks to his critics to be a wishful thinker, and in times of stress to be either pig-headed or self-deceiving. This is perhaps why it is this element of inappositeness to the evidence that is so prominent in the non-religious use of 'faith'; and it is perhaps a vague awareness of the element of personal loyalty in religious faith that generates the moderately complimentary overtones of the term in secular contexts. It has of course been one of the major burdens of this book that we can produce a more comprehending account of what religious faith is than the common sceptical account which just regards it as identical in structure to non-religious faith - and that we can do this without committing ourselves in the process to the truth of the propositions the man of faith holds. Our account is not refuted if it should turn out that believers and sceptics, in speaking of faith, sometimes talk at cross-purposes.

Appendix B: Pascal's Wager

I have said in the text that emphasis on the importance of Christian claims can be used with equal ease by the critics of those claims and by their supporters. The most famous attempt to use it made by a Christian apologist is Pascal's 'Wager' argument (1). I shall not attempt to examine it in detail here, but there is one common misunderstanding of it that has bearing upon the argument of this book.

Pascal's argument is in essence an appeal to the prudence or self-interest of a sceptic. It should not be taken without careful exegesis as following from other things he says in the

'Pensées', which is a complex and unfinished work. Pascal takes it as given in the Wager argument that reason cannot decide for us whether or not Christian claims are true. In these circumstances considerations of *prudence* ought to move the sceptic to change his position. In famous passages elsewhere in the 'Pensées', Pascal makes very clear his own commitment to the revelatory character of much of human experience, and of special Christian proclamations; but in the Wager passage he is self-consciously appealing only to those considerations that might still remain to influence a sceptic after the usual appeals to allegedly revelatory phenomena, or to purported proofs, have been rejected. In this passage he is, in my terms, assuming the truth of theological non-naturalism, and trying to offer the one remaining rational appeal that is still open to him. He realises that to the sceptic the standard appeals to revelation and Christian rites will properly seem mere resorts to persuasive devices; but he offers a reason for yielding to them nevertheless. The reason is that in a situation where reason cannot decide the truth of the Christian claims, it is the importance of these claims that should be the determining factor. If these claims are true, then disbelieving them will result in eternal damnation, whereas accepting them will yield salvation. If they are false, nothing is lost by having held them to be true. So unbelief is foolishness. The only prudent course for the sceptic is to follow those devices that will induce the belief that has so far not implanted itself: by taking holy water, having masses said, and in general acting as if one believed.

There have been both sound and unsound objections to this argument. One unsound one needs to be attacked here. It is mentioned, with apparent approval, by William James, in his far inferior essay 'The Will to Believe' (2). James urges against Pascal that 'a faith in masses and holy water adopted wilfully after such calculation would lack the inner soul of faith's reality'. This misses the point. Pascal's point is that someone without faith would do well, considering matters prudentially, to acquire it. But what this says he should acquire is the genuine article, not some simulation of it. The rituals are to be adopted in the first instance not because following them *is* faith, but because following them may *induce* faith. If it does not materialise, these devices have not

156

worked. If James is merely saying that they will not work, what makes him so sure? If they would not, would some others? The question this objection of James's raises for us is whether faith, as we have described it, is something that can be induced by psychological means. Given that faith is a state of mind, however complex, and that states of mind have psychological causes, there can be no grounds for denying *a priori* the logical possibility of discovering what these have been in the case of others and trying to use this as a way of inducing it in oneself or one's friends. It would be idle to deny that the preacher or the missionary use such knowledge in their work. Why should they not? If it is said that faith is not a form of prudence, the answer again is that Pascal has not suggested that it is. He has merely suggested that prudence is a ground for acquiring faith; obviously when faith has been acquired it will not itself be a prudential state of mind.

Some might feel that the very suggestion that faith could be something that one man might learn how to induce in another, or induce in himself, is a ground for giving faith a specifically theological definition, of the sort we discussed in Chapter 6, so that faith is in logic something that only God could induce in someone. There is, however, no advantage in this insistence unless one is prepared to deny that divine grace reaches men through human actions and choices and psychological states, or is prepared to deny that faith can be recognised to exist by those who do not have it. For if either of these is admitted, faith becomes once again a proper object for psychology to study.

Hick argues briefly against Pascal that the Wager argument reduces the adoption of faith to the self-protecting pro-pitiation of a vengeful deity (3). In part this seems similar to James's objection, and the response to it is that it confuses the motive for seeking to acquire faith when one lacks it, with the nature of faith itself when one has it. In any case, would there not be an element of vengefulness in a des-cription of God which entailed that a man seeking faith for selfish reasons could never acquire it? One of the real difficulties in the Wager argument lies in the doctrine of eternal punishment itself, and Hick is right to touch upon this. Without a cosmic scheme that includes eternal damnation, there is no basis for the Wager argument, for there is then nothing in the doctrine to generate the prudential considerations on which it depends. But if one includes a doctrine of eternal punishment within the Christian scheme that the sceptic is asked to consider, then one is recommending that he acquire a faith in which he willingly accepts and praises a cosmic economy in which men are damned for unbelief. In a world in which theological non-naturalism is true and unbelief reasonable, this cosmic economy would not merit the praise accorded to it. But in a world in which theological non-naturalism were *not* true, and proofs could be had, reason could decide on Christian claims on other grounds, and the evidential vacuum in which the Wager comes into play would not exist (4).

Appendix C: Hume on Miracles

The concept of a miracle and the concept of a sign are not identical. While some alleged signs are alleged miracles, not all are. Some brief comments on Hume's discussion of the epistemology of the miraculous (1) is nevertheless in order here, in view of my remarks on the extent to which the believer and the unbeliever may have identical expectations concerning the course of the world, and on the drawbacks of our dependence on testimony in learning of the formative events of the Christian tradition.

Two points, both stressed by commentators(2), are essential for the evaluation of Hume's essay. The first is that whatever incidental insights can be had about his general attitudes to religious belief from the tone of his discussion, the basic thrust of his argument is to discredit attempts to use alleged miraculous happenings to form the foundation of a system of religion: in other words, Hume considers he has refuted arguments that begin from such happenings and proceed from them, after the manner of natural theology, to theistic conclusions. His argument does not necessarily have force against reasoning about miracles that begins from theistic premises. The second is that he takes it for granted that the evidence we have for the miraculous is confined to testimony.

In the briefest summary, his argument is as follows. A wise

158

man proportions his belief to the evidence. A miracle is a violation of the laws of nature, and therefore an event which past experience is uniformly against. This in itself makes it overwhelmingly probable that the miracle did not occur, unless the testimony to it is of such superlative quality that it can seriously be weighed against such uniform past experience. In fact, however, the testimony for miracles is not of this quality at all: the standard of the witnesses has not been high, the human capacity for accepting the unlikely has all too probably been at work, the tales related derive from 'ignorant and barbarous' places and nations, and in any case the miracle-stories of competing religions cancel each other out. Consequently testimony to miracles can never establish them so that one could proceed, from a proper assurance that they have occurred, to infer some theistic conclusion. In my language, no non-theistic premiss which reports an event contrary to natural law could ever be so well established by testimony that we could properly claim to know its truth and then infer some theistic conclusion from it.

Critics have pointed out that Hume's argument does not allow for the accumulated impact of repeated testimony to one and the same event. More importantly, they have emphasised that it does nothing to undermine the assurance of someone who witnesses some event contrary to the laws of nature, rather than hears of it through testimony. In spite of this, it seems to me, as to many other readers, that Hume's case is decisive against its central target: that is, against any attempted proof of a theistic conclusion that bases itself on a non-theistic premiss which reports an event contrary to natural law and is supported by testimony. For if one confines oneself in assessing it to the likelihoods that we learn from our experience of nature, such testimony ought to be rejected. Hence it is quite in accord with the ordinary canons of evidence for sceptics to reject the gospel miracle-stories, and to reject claims made by believers that God has intervened in nature at other times.

But the believer's position is not the same. He already considers himself to know some truths about God's nature and relation to men. Consequently he is not confined, as the sceptic is, to ordinary inductive considerations when assessing testimony to allegedly miraculous events. He has to bring his supposed knowledge of God to bear, as well as these inductive considerations. In the light of this evaluation, he may quite reasonably decide differently about the likelihood of the testimony being true. There is nothing in Hume's argument to make it unreasonable for someone who already knows certain things about God to decide that on some occasion God has indeed intervened in the world. So although the believer may have the same views about the course of nature and history that the sceptic has, he need not have.

But if he wishes to combine his religious beliefs with a modern acceptance of scientific knowledge, he will have the same expectations and historical opinions as the sceptic. Believers do not need to hold there are any miracles, as long as they hold that there are either some revelatory events or some natural events which make it overwhelmingly probable that God exists. But they can, in practice, hold that there are *some* miracles. The position of many believers seems to be roughly as follows. They believe that some miracles have occurred, but not many. Ninian Smart (3) points out that although a miracle is thought of as a violation of natural law, it is not thought of by believers as an anomalous event that undermines the status of the law: it is thought to be an event which represents a temporary suspension of the law on the part of God, so that apart from this theologically significant happening, the natural law remains in force. So the believer does not expect (for example) any more virgin births, or resurrections; or at least, he is not committed to this by his belief that each of these has occurred once on God's intervention. If he thinks of miracles this way, he can coexist in scientific matters with sceptics quite easily, for the miraculous events he believes in and the sceptic rejects do not affect their attitudes to scientific understanding in general. This peaceful coexistence can continue on two conditions. One is that the believer, though holding there have been some miracles, does not think there have been many of them; they must be rare. The other is that the miracles he does hold to are learned about in ways which he is able to see that the sceptic must, in fullest reason, reject. I do not speculate how many of these ways there can be. But certainly the major one, and possibly the only one, is through testimony.

160

Knowing what he thinks he knows, the believer can reasonably accept testimony; but he can equally well see the sceptic must reject it. The believer will have to have some standard, based no doubt on normative revelations, to enable him to decide which testimony there is a prior theological likelihood of being sound and which not; and there are many difficulties here when traditions compete, as Hume saw. But it is possible for him to accept some testimony without his doing so affecting his epistemological coexistence with the sceptic in other matters. They can disagree about a *small number* of miracle-stories, such as those of the post-Resurrection appearances, and agree about the way the world goes the rest of the time. The deadlock is unaffected, and is not epistemologically hazardous outside religious contexts, as the coexistence of Christian and atheist scientists and historians makes plain.

The deadlock could of course be broken. It could be broken if a miracle, or some other sign, were to occur, and were to be witnessed by the sceptic and the believer alike. Then of course the sceptic might still deny it: one is able even to doubt the testimony of one's own senses if one tries. But the stance he would then assume would not be a rational one, and the deadlock would then be one he could be blamed for. If this happened, theological non-naturalism would be false. It does not, however, seem to be.

Notes

CHAPTER 1

1. The two best-known sources for debate about scepticism of meaning are Antony Flew and Alasdair MacIntyre (eds), 'New Essays in Philosophical Theology' (S.C.M. Press, 1955), and Basil Mitchell (ed.), 'Faith and Logic' (Allen & Unwin, 1957).

2. See Part II of my 'Religion and Rationality' (New York: Random House, forthcoming).

3. See Kai Nielsen's paper of this title in 'Philosophy', xlii (1967) pp. 191–209. See especially D. Z. Phillips (ed.), 'Religion and Understanding' (Oxford: Blackwell, 1967).

4. See the essay 'Understanding a Primitive Society' by Peter Winch, in D. Z. Phillips, op. cit., pp. 9–42, and Alasdair MacIntyre, 'Is Understanding Religion Compatible with Believing?', in John Hick (ed.), 'Faith and the Philosophers', (New York: St Martin's Press, 1964) pp. 115–33.

5. See Part I of 'Religion and Rationality',

6. 'Summa Theologica', Part I, Question 1, Article 8 ad 2.

7. See John Hick, 'Faith and Knowledge', 2nd ed. (Ithaca, N.Y.: Cornell Univ. Press, 1966) pp. 16–20.

8. 'Summa Theologica', IIa IIae, Q.4 Art. 8.

9. 'Summa Theologica', IIa IIae, Q.2 Art. 5 ad 2.

10. 'Of Revelation' from the translation by Cardinal Manning of the Decrees of the First Vatican Council. These are conveniently reproduced as an Appendix to Geddes MacGregor, 'The Vatican Revolution' (Macmillan, 1958).

11. John Hick, op. cit.

12. See Hick's article 'Faith' in Paul Edwards (ed.), 'Encyclopedia of Philosophy' (New York: Macmillan, (1967) iii 165–9.

13. Ludwig Wittgenstein, 'Philosophical Investigations', trans. G. E. M. Anscombe (Oxford: Blackwell, 1953) II xi 193 ff.

14. John Hick, 'Religious Faith as Experiencing-As' in G. N. A. Vesey (ed.), 'Talk of God', Royal Institute of Philosophy Lectures, vol. 2, 1967–8 (Macmillan, 1969) pp. 20–35.

CHAPTER 2

1. This is not intended to imply, either, that the contrast between revelation and proof needs no examination. See Chapter 5.

2. This was originally published in the 'Proceedings of the British Academy', xxv (1939), and is reprinted in G. E. Moore, 'Philosophical Papers' (Allen & Unwin, 1959) pp. 127–50. References here are to the latter.

3. Ibid., pp. 145–6.

4. Moore makes what I take to be the same point with another example. He says that proofs of the sort that he has given are commonly taken to be satisfactory, and instances a dispute where what is in question is whether or not there are at least three misprints on a certain page. The man who says there are could prove it by pointing to three places on the page, and saying each time that there is a misprint in that place. This would be an adequate proof provided it is 'certain' that there is a misprint in each place pointed to. I take it that part of the point of this additional example is that 'There are at least three misprints on the page' is proved by means of the premiss 'Here is one misprint and here is another misprint and here is a third misprint', provided this premiss is known to be true, even though the premiss is not itself proved to be true. The point of concern in my argument is the claim that in a good proof all that is requisite is that the premiss is known to be true, not that it be known in some particular way rather than another. I am not concerned here with Moore's basic insistence that one can make it known by pointing it out; only with his insistence that its being known, rather than its being known in some particular way, is all that is required in one's account of what a proof is. See Moore, op. cit., p. 147.

5. Moore, op. cit., p. 146. His actual words are these:

But did I prove just now that two human hands were then in existence? I do want to insist that I did; that the proof which I gave was a perfectly rigorous one; and that it is perhaps impossible to give a better or more rigorous proof of anything whatever. Of course, it would not have been a proof unless three conditions were satisfied; namely (1)

163

unless the premiss which I adduced as proof of the conclusion was different from the conclusion I adduced it to prove; (2) unless the premiss which I adduced was something which I *knew* to be the case, and not merely something which I believed but which was by no means certain, or something which, though in fact true, I did not know to be so; and (3) unless the conclusion did really follow from the premiss. But all these three conditions were in fact satisfied by my proof. (p. 146)

6. This expression is used by George I. Mavrodes in chap. ii of 'Belief in God' (New York: Random House, 1970) p. 40. Although my conclusions differ from his, I am much indebted throughout to his very original discussion of the enterprise of proving the existence of God, which I was first privileged to hear in an earlier version.

7. For a detailed account of the relationship between them, see chap. 1, and Part I of chap. 2, of P. F. Strawson, 'Introduction to Logical Theory' (Methuen, 1952).

8. These are from an unpublished paper, 'True Statements and Discursive Proofs', which was read to the Western Division of the American Philosophical Association in May 1961.

9. I owe this useful distinction to some comments of Mr Stuart C. Brown. He is not guilty of suggesting this particular application of it.

10. For discussions of the meaning and the strengths and weaknesses of the Ontological Proof, the reader is recommended to consult two anthologies: John Hick and Arthur C. McGill (eds) 'The Many-Faced Argument' (New York: Macmillan, 1967), and Alvin Plantinga (ed.), 'The Ontological Argument' (Garden City, N.Y.: Doubleday, 1965). See also E. L. Mascall, 'Faith and Reason: Anselm and Aquinas', in 'Journal of Theological Studies', new series, xiv (1) (1963), and Karl Barth, 'Anselm: Fides Quaerens Intellectum', trans. Ian W. Robertson (S.C.M. Press, 1960).

11. See Appendix A.

12. James F. Ross, 'Philosophical Theology' (New York: Bobbs-Merrill, 1969) p. 15.

13. G. E. Moore, 'Hume's Philosophy', in 'Philosophical Studies' (Kegan Paul, Trench, Trubner & Co., 1922). See

also the comments on reversing arguments in J. J. C. Smart, 'The Existence of God', in Antony Flew and Alasdair MacIntyre (eds), 'New Essays in Philosophical Theology' (S.C.M. Press, 1955).

14. This is so, at least, if the mechanism of self-deception works and the previous knowledge is smothered.

15. Since the text of Hume's 'Dialogues' is not quite unequivocal on this matter, my interpretation may seem to need argument. In the fifth paragraph of Part II, Cleanthes expounds his argument, laying primary stress upon the analogy between the 'machines' of which the natural world is composed, and the products of human design. He concludes with the sentence, 'By this argument *a posteriori*, and by this argument alone, do we prove at once the existence of a Deity and his similarity to human mind and intelligence'. Demea, one of whose functions is to represent supporters of the *a priori* arguments, objects as follows: 'What! No demonstration of the Being of God! No abstract arguments! No proofs *a priori*! ...Can we reach no farther in this subject than experience and probability?' Philo, on the other hand, complains 'not so much that all religious arguments are by Cleanthes reduced to experience, as that they appear not to be even the most certain and irrefragable of that inferior kind'.

A precise interpretation of this three-cornered dispute is difficult, especially if one does not correctly judge the degree of irony in that last 'inferior'. But it is not necessary. Although Hume's theory of knowledge as expounded in Section IV of the 'Enquiry' requires him to confine certainty in the conclusions of arguments to the conclusions of deductive demonstrations *a priori*, thus excluding all matters of fact, the probability which he has Cleanthes assign to the conclusion of his argument is the highest degree which arguments from experience can yield. As an argument from experience Cleanthes holds his argument to be far better than average; Philo says it is poorer than average. Cleanthes, in assigning it this status, calls it a proof; Philo does not deny it is correct to call it an attempted one.

CHAPTER 3

1. J. N. Findlay, 'Can God's Existence Be Disproved?', in 'Mind' (1948), reprinted with rejoinders by G. E. Hughes and A. C. A. Rainer in Antony Flew and Alasdair MacIntyre (eds), 'New Essays in Philosophical Theology' (S.C.M. Press, 1955) pp. 47–75.

2. See, for discussions, Nelson Pike (ed.), 'God and Evil' (Englewood Cliffs, N.J.: Prentice-Hall, 1964); John Hick, 'Evil and the God of Love' (Macmillan, 1966); Edward H. Madden and Peter H. Hare, 'Evil and the Concept of God' (Springfield, Ill.: Charles C. Thomas, 1968).

3. For a comment on the nature of the problem, see my 'Divine Goodness and the Problem of Evil', in 'Religious Studies', ii (1966) 95–107. For wider comments, see chaps. 16 and 17 of 'Religion and Rationality'.

4. David Hume, 'Enquiry Concerning Human Understanding', Section IV, part 1, first sentence.

5. Alasdair MacIntyre, 'The Logical Status of Religious Belief', in MacIntyre (ed.), 'Metaphysical Beliefs' (S.C.M. Press, 1957) p. 209.

6. John Hick, 'Christianity at the Centre' (S.C.M. Press, 1968) pp. 55–6.

7. Hick, 'Faith and Knowledge', chap. 6.

8. See MacIntyre, op. cit., pp. 202–3; also D. Z. Phillips, 'The Concept of Prayer' (Routledge & Kegan Paul, 1965) chap. 1; the same author's 'Faith, Scepticism, and Religious Understanding', in D. Z. Phillips (ed.), 'Religion and Understanding' (Oxford: Blackwell, 1967) pp. 63–80; and the debate between Hick, Humphrey Palmer, and Phillips in 'Theology', lxxi (1968) 100–22.

9. P. F. Strawson, 'On Referring', in 'Mind', lix (1950) 320–44. Reprinted in G. H. R. Parkinson (ed.), 'The Theory of Meaning' (Oxford University Press, 1968) pp. 61–85. My indebtedness to this classic paper is obvious throughout this section.

10. Gareth B. Matthews, 'Theology and Natural Theology', in 'Journal of Philosophy', lxi (1964) 99–108.

11. It is worthy of note that some apparently non-theistic premisses that have been alleged to prove theistic conclusions have been statements of a high degree of metaphysical

generality. In our own day such principles have less initial appeal to most philosophers than the theistic conclusions they have been thought to support, but one never knows where philosophy will go next.

12. See Appendix B.

13. See Appendix C.

CHAPTER 4

1. See chap. 8 of 'Faith and Knowledge' and the article 'Theology and Verification', in 'Theology Today', xvii (1960) 12–31.

2. For general accounts of the disputes surrounding this principle, see J. O. Urmson, 'Philosophical Analysis: Its Development Between the Two World Wars' (Oxford University Press, 1956); W.P. Alston, 'Philosophy of Language' (Englewood Cliffs, N.J.: Prentice-Hall, 1964) chap. 4; Carl G. Hempel, 'Problems and Changes in the Empiricist Criterion of Meaning', in 'Revue Internationale de Philosophie' (1950); reprinted in C. G. Hempel, 'Aspects of Scientific Explanation' (New York: Free Press of Glencoe, 1966).

3. A. J. Ayer, 'Language, Truth, and Logic' (Gollancz, 1936).

4. The best-known attack upon it is Norman Malcolm, 'The Verification Argument', in Max Black (ed.), 'Philosophical Analysis' (Ithaca, N.Y.: Cornell U.P., 1950) pp. 244–98.

5. I mean by this that it is entirely in accord with the common use of 'verify' and its cognates to admit the possibility of a statement's being verified by the acquisition of knowledge which, when expressed in statements, does not entail it. I do not mean that there cannot be a case where the statements that express the verification of another statement also entail it; though Hick appears to hold this.

6. Although it does not bear upon our main concerns, there seems nothing wrong in the suggestion that one can verify necessary truths. An obvious example would be someone's verifying his belief that the square root of 108, 171 is 329 by a piece of elementary multiplication, or verifying his vague recollection that in any right-angled triangle the area of

the squares on the hypotenuse is equal to the sum of the areas of the squares on the other two sides by working through the Pythagorean proof. This last example shows that it is a mistake to think that verification and proof are exclusive concepts. In some contexts they may be readily interchangeable; in others one may speak, as here, of verifying something by proving it; though it does seem odder to speak of proving something by verifying it.

7. See Paul van Buren, 'The Secular Meaning of the Gospel' (S.C.M. Press, 1963); John A. T. Robinson, 'Honest to God' (S.C.M. Press, 1963); B. Murchland (ed.), 'The Meaning of the Death of God' (New York: Vintage Books, Random House, 1967); R. B. Braithwaite, 'An Empiricist's View of the Nature of Religious Belief', Eddington Memorial Lecture (Cambridge University Press, 1955), reprinted in I.T. Ramsey (ed), 'Christian Ethics and Contemporary Philosophy' (S.C.M. Press, 1966) pp. 53–73. For a conservative critique, see E. L. Mascall, 'The Secularisation of Christianity' (Longmans, 1965).

8. See his 'Systematic Theology', 3 vols (University of Chicago Press, 1951, 1957, 1963).

9. See David Cox, 'The Significance of Christianity', in 'Mind', lx (1950) pp. 209-18.

10. See Antony Flew and Alasdair MacIntyre (eds), 'New Essays in Philosophical Theology' (S.C.M. Press, 1955) pp. 96–130.

11. See note 1 above.

12. For a discussion of these and references to other works, see my 'Survival and Disembodied Existence' (Routledge & Kegan Paul, 1970).

13. This charge is made in R. W. Hepburn, 'From World to God', in 'Mind' lxxii (1963) 40–50.

14. It is this problem to which the Thomistic doctrine of analogical prediction is an attempted answer. I comment on it in chap. 12 of 'Religion and Rationality' (New York: Random House, forthcoming).

15. He presents it as a possible (and orthodox) view, not as his own.

16. 'Faith and Knowledge', pp. 192 f.

CHAPTER 5

1. See Appendix C.

2. This is the common philosophical title for the mistake involved in thinking that a point of view has been discredited when it has been shown to have embarrassing origins. Such information does not affect the question of its truth, though it may make us more censorious about those who hold it.

3. See the article by W. P. Alston ('Religion, Psychological Explanations of') and R. W. Hepburn ('Religious Experience, Argument for the Existence of God') in Paul Edwards's 'Encyclopedia of Philosophy', vii (New York: Macmillan, 1967); also Alston's contribution to John Hick (ed.), 'Faith and the Philosophers' (Macmillan, 1964) pp. 63–102.

4. This restriction cannot be followed entirely, as will become clear by the end of this chapter. See also Appendix C.

5. I take this phrase from H. D. Lewis, 'Our Experience of God' (Allen & Unwin, 1959) p. 149.

6. Appendix C.

7. E. L. Mascall tends at times to suggest this, especially in 'Existence and Analogy' (Longmans, 1949).

8. See 'Religion and Rationality', chap. 6 (New York: Random House, forthcoming).

9. R. W. Hepburn, 'Christianity and Paradox' (Watts, 1958) pp. 204–8.

10. H. D. Lewis, 'Our Experience of God' (Allen & Unwin, 1959) pp. 99–103.

11. Certain forms of radical theology, as found in Bultmann or Van Buren, look as though they provide exceptions to this, since they seem willing to rest content with a deep scepticism about the historicity of the gospel records. But a consequence of this scepticism is their willingness to rest content also with the view that what is revelatory is the tradition of the Church, or the Church itself as a historical community, rather than the primary events to which the Church witnesses; or even, if I interpret the latter correctly, to dispense with the requirement of God's existence, and hence with the concept of revelation itself. We are likely then to end with a version of what I have called Theological Phenomenalism. See H. Bartsch (ed.), 'Kerygma

and Myth' (New York: Harper, 1961); Paul van Buren, 'The Secular Meaning of the Gospel' (S.C.M. Press, 1963).

12. This seems to be the view of John Baillie. See 'Our Knowledge of God' (New York: Scribner's, 1959), and the Epilogue to 'The Idea of Revelation in Recent Thought' (New York: Columbia U.P., 1956).

13. 'The Idea of Revelation in Recent Thought', p. 64.

14. See the Hepburn - Lewis controversy once again.

15. See chaps. iv and v of Baillie's 'The Idea of Revelation in Recent Thought'. The logical point that revelation is person-relative does not detract, or need not detract, from doctrines that some normative revelatory phenomenon, such as the life of Christ, is for all mankind, or has taken place once and for all. These expressions may merely emphasise that it is this unique phenomenon, and no other, which is the one to which a man must respond for revelation to occur, or for other revelatory phenomena to be interpreted correctly. Others may have subsidiary significance and the theology must allow space for the responses of men at later times to the primary phenomenon.

16. A man's position may have excellent reasons to support it even if he has discreditable motives for wanting it to be true.

CHAPTER 6

1. In my terminology, 'Christians believe that all men are sinners' is a non-theistic statement, but one which contains theistic expressions.

2. A similar decision would have to be made if someone attempted to produce a religiously neutral analysis of the concept of 'worship'. To say that someone worships a certain being need not be interpreted as implying that the speaker himself accepts the existence of a being with the qualities justifying such veneration. It could just mean that the worshipper takes there to be a being endowed with these qualities. But if this is said to be of the essence of worship, then heathen adoration of idols, and, most especially, secular veneration of cult-heroes and of the State, should not be admitted to be cases of worship at all, without great care being exercised. The advisability of using the term would

probably depend on how far the cases of quasi-worship entailed ascribing to their objects attributes like those ascribed in the full-blooded cases.

3. Not all causal accounts of the origins or effects of faith carry this entailment. The man of faith does not have to deny the effects of his personal history on his present state of mind, or the effects the latter will have on his actions. Such investigations could form the subject-matter of social science, and do. The sceptic will go further than this, and will use such neutral explanation to explain faith away.

4. This would have the awkward result that adherence to Christian heresies could not even be examples of faith.

5. This is argued on behalf of faith in chap. 9 of Hick's 'Faith and Knowledge', but it surely works for scepticism too.

6. Chap. 11 of 'Religion and Rationality'.

7. The contrast between faith and sight is one which it is natural to express by saying that faith is indirect knowledge of that which will be known directly at a later time. There are some hazards for us in this. I have made use of a distinction between direct and indirect proof, and of a corresponding distinction between direct and indirect verification. A form of direct proof, if we wish to use the notion, would be that of perceiving the state of affairs which someone has asserted to obtain. Here what is asserted and what is perceived is that p. Similarly, to use our example of the storekeeper again, we could directly verify that a certain sum is in the till by looking and seeing that this is so. Indirect proof and verification involve inferring that p from some other, prior knowledge, that q. The claim that men will know God face to face might well be put by saying that they will know of him directly; but it is hazardous to infer from this that the knowledge the man of faith considers himself to have is therefore indirect. If it comes through proof (in the way in which proof is on my account available to him) it will be indirect, doubtless. But if it comes from alleged revelation this is not so clear. In revelation we do have some phenomenon, reportable in the non-theistic statement, q, through which the believer considers he has come to know that p. If the fact of q were offered as a reason for holding that p, as in the case of proof, the language of indirect knowledge would

be clearly appropriate - and if there were probative revelations, q could be offered successfully as a conclusive reason
for p. But alleged revelations do not occur in this manner;
indeed, although in logic the separation of p and q is always
possible, those who consider they have received revelation
may not even be able with clarity to effect the separation.
They may, even if they do make it, consider, contrary to the
sceptic, that they have one phenomenon under two descriptions. There is therefore some grounds to hesitate in the
case of revelation to use the language of indirect knowledge.
On this, see the acute comments of Mavrodes in 'Belief in
God', chap. iii.

8. Hick, 'Faith and Knowledge', p. 209.

9. There is no reason to deny that a corresponding judgement can be made about the sceptic's position. The analogy
is not exact, of course, because of the very absence of anything corresponding to the factor of revelation. But if the
sceptic claims to know either that God does not exist, or that
no one can know that he does, then, if he appeals to the
standard of economy, or insists upon sensory verification
here and now as a criterion of knowledge of matters of fact,
and God in fact does not exist (and *a fortiori* no one can
know that he does), he has based his claim to knowledge on
the only correct standard and presumably his claim has to be
accepted. The only snag, once again, is that we cannot determine that it *is* correct independently of rejecting what it
excludes. There is even a partial analogue to some religious
experience that is accessible to the sceptic, viz. the revulsion
some sceptics feel from Christianity as a system of pre-
posterous primitive fantasies, or the sense of liberation some
sceptics experience when contemplating the picture of the
world as a wholly secular material system. Such experiences,
if the judgements they embody are true, have an equivalent
right to be classified as cognitive ones.

10. This is argued by Alasdair MacIntyre in 'The Logical
Status of Religious Belief', section iii, p. 180—5.

11. To deny this is to end up equating faith with serious-
ness. This form of theological phenomenalism is found in
Paul Tillich's 'Dynamics of Faith' (New York: Harper, 1957).

12. 'Faith and Knowledge', pp. 19—21.

13. For a good recent discussion of this Socratic conten-

tion, see Gerasimos Santas, 'The Socratic Paradoxes', in 'Philosophical Review' lxxiii (1964) 147—64, reprinted in A. Sesonske and N. Fleming (eds), 'Plato's Meno' (Belmont, California: Wadsworth, 1965) pp. 49—64.

14. John Hick, 'Religious Faith as Experiencing—As', in G. N. A. Vesey (ed.), 'Talk of God', Royal Institute of Philosophy Lectures, vol. 2, 1967—8 (Macmillan, 1969) pp. 20—35.

APPENDIX A

1. Terence Penelhum, 'Pleasure and Falsity', in 'American Philosophical Quarterly', (1964) 1—11; reprinted in Stuart Hampshire (ed.), 'Philosophy of Mind' (New York: Harper & Row, 1966) pp. 242—66.

2. John V. Canfield and Don F. Gustavson, 'Self-Deception', in 'Analysis' xxiii (1962) 32—6.

3. Herbert Fingarette, 'Self-Deception' (London: Routledge & Kegan Paul; New York: Humanities Press, 1969) pp. 23—33.

4. Patrick Gardiner, 'Error, Faith, and Self-Deception', in 'Proceedings of the Aristotelian Society' (1969—70) pp. 221—43.

APPENDIX B

1. The Wager argument can be found as fragment no. 233 in the first Everyman edition, trans. W.F. Trotter (London: J. M. Dent; New York: E. P. Dutton, 1908); in the newer Everyman edition, trans. John Warrington (1960), where it is fragment no. 343. It is no. 223 in the convenient H. F. Stewart bilingual edition, published by Random House, New York.

2. William James, 'The Will to Believe and Other Essays' (New York: Longmans, Green 1897).

3. John Hick, 'Faith and Knowledge', pp. 33—5.

4. I have attempted to deal with the Wager argument more fully in 'Pascal's Wager', in 'Journal of Religion', xliv (1964) 201—9, and in chap. 15 of 'Religion and Rationality'.

1. David Hume, 'An Enquiry Concerning Human Understanding', Section X, many editions.

2. The best commentators are C. D. Broad, 'Hume's Theory of the Credibility of Miracles', in 'Proceedings of the Aristotelian Society', xvii (1916—17) 77—94, reprinted in Sesonske and Fleming (eds), 'Human Understanding' (Belmont, Calif.: Wadsworth, 1965); and Antony Flew, 'Hume's Philosophy of Belief' (Routledge & Kegan Paul, 1961) chap. viii.

3. Ninian Smart, 'Philosophers and Religious Truth', 2nd ed. (S.C.M. Press, 1969) chap. ii.

Select Bibliography

No bibliography on topics like faith or revelation can claim to be complete. The works listed here are mostly recent, and all are available in English. An asterisk indicates that the book or article so marked has been cited in the text. The notation '(B)' indicates that the work includes a useful bibliography that goes beyond the present one.

I. General Works

This list includes recent books and articles that explore, from varying viewpoints, the rationality of religious belief, and the relationship of philosophical inquiry to it.

Renford Bambrough, 'Reason, Truth, and God' (London: Methuen; New York: Barnes & Noble, 1969).

Stuart C. Brown, 'Do Religious Claims Make Sense?' (S.C.M. Press, 1969).

Antony Flew, 'God and Philosophy' (Hutchinson, 1966), (B).

Ronald W. Hepburn, 'Christianity and Paradox' (London: Watts, 1958; New York: Pegasus, 1966).

*John Hick, 'Christianity at the Centre' (S.C.M. Press, 1968).

*John Hick, 'Faith and Knowledge', 2nd ed. (Ithaca, N.Y.: Cornell U.P., 1966).

C. B. Martin, 'Religious Belief' (Ithaca, N.Y.: Cornell U.P., 1959).

*George I. Mavrodes, 'Belief in God' (New York: Random House, 1970).

Terence Penelhum, 'Religion and Rationality' (New York: Random House, forthcoming, probably 1971).

Alvin Plantinga, 'God and Other Minds' (Ithaca, N.Y.: Cornell, U.P., 1967).

Richard Robinson, 'An Atheist's Values' (Oxford University Press, 1964).

*James F. Ross, 'Philosophical Theology' (Indianapolis and New York: Bobbs-Merrill, 1969).

Ninian Smart, 'Philosophers and Religious Truth', 2nd ed. (S.C.M. Press, 1969).

Ninian Smart, 'Reasons and Faiths' (Routledge & Kegan Paul, 1958).

Ronald W. Hepburn, 'From World to God', in 'Mind', lxxii (1963) 40—50.

*Alasdair MacIntyre, 'The Logical Status of Religious Belief', in A. MacIntyre (ed.), 'Metaphysical Beliefs' (S.C.M. Press, 1957).

Basil Mitchell, 'Neutrality and Commitment', Inaugural Lecture, University of Oxford (Oxford University Press, 1968).

A. N. Prior, 'Can Religion Be Discussed?', in Antony Flew and Alasdair MacIntyre (eds), 'New Essays in Philosophical Theology' (Methuen, 1955) pp. 1—11; reprinted from 'Australasian Journal of Philosophy' (1942).

II. Works on the Topics of Particular Chapters

Chapter 1

Scepticism of meaning

I. M. Crombie, 'The Possibility of Theological Statements', in Basil Mitchell (ed.), 'Faith and Logic' (Allen & Unwin, 1957) pp. 31—83.

Frederick Ferré, 'Language, Logic, and God' (Eyre & Spottiswoode, 1962).

Antony Flew, et al., 'Theology and Falsification', in Flew and MacIntyre, 'New Essays in Philosophical Theology', pp. 96—130.

Alasdair MacIntyre, 'Is Understanding Religion Compatible with Believing?', in John Hick (ed.), 'Faith and the Philosophers' (London: Macmillan; New York: St Martin's Press, 1964) pp. 115—33.

Terence Penelhum, 'Religion and Rationality', Part II.

Ian T. Ramsey, 'Religious Language' (S.C.M. Press, 1957).

Wittgensteinian fideism

John Hick, 'The Justification of Religious Belief', in 'Theology', lxxi (1968) 100—7.

Norman Malcolm, 'Anselm's Ontological Arguments', in

'Philosophical Review'. lxix (1960) 41—62; reprinted in D. Z. Phillips,'Religion and Understanding' (see below).

Kai Nielsen, 'Wittgensteinian Fideism', in 'Philosophy', xlii (1967) 00—00.

Humphrey Palmer, 'Understanding First', in 'Theology', lxxi (1968) 107—14.

D. Z. Phillips, 'The Concept of Prayer' (Routledge & Kegan Paul, 1965).

D. Z. Phillips, 'Faith, Scepticism and Religious Understanding', in D. Z. Phillips (ed.), 'Religion and Understanding' (Oxford: Blackwell, 1967) pp. 63—80.

D. Z. Phillips, 'Religious Belief and Philosophical Enquiry', in 'Theology', lxxi (1968) 114—22.

Peter Winch, 'Understanding a Primitive Society', in D. Z. Phillips (ed), 'Religion and Understanding', pp. 9—42.

Ludwig Wittgenstein, 'Lectures and Conversations on Aesthetics, Psychology and Religious Belief', ed. Cyril Barrett (Oxford: Blackwell, 1966).

Two accounts of faith

Aquinas, 'Summa Theologica', Secunda Secundae, Questions 1—7. Available in the translation of the 'Summa' by the Fathers of the English Dominican Province (London: Burns, Oates & Washbourne; New York: Benziger Bros, 1947). The translation quoted in the text is that of A.M. Fairweather, in 'Nature and Grace', Selections from the Summa Theologica of St Thomas Aquinas, The Library of Christian Classics, xi (London: S.C.M. Press; Philadelphia: Westminster Press, 1954).

For St Thomas's distinction between natural and revealed theology, see 'Summa Theologica', Part I, Questions 1 and 2, and 'Summa Contra Gentiles', Book 1, chaps. 1—12. The 'Summa Contra Gentiles' is available in a translation by Anton C. Pegis et al., entitled 'On the Truth of the Catholic Faith' (New York: Doubleday, 1955).

John Hick, 'Faith', in 'Encyclopedia of Philosophy', ed Paul Edwards (New York: Macmillan, 1967) iii 165—9 (B).

*John Hick, 'Faith and Knowledge', 2nd ed. (Ithaca, N.Y.: Cornell U.P., 1966).

*John Hick, 'Religious Faith as Experiencing-As', in G. N. A.

Vesey (ed.), 'Talk of God', Royal Institute of Philosophy
Lectures, vol. 2, 1967—8 (London: Macmillan; New York:
St Martin's Press, 1969) pp. 20—35.

Chapters 2 and 3

Moore's proof

*G. E. Moore, 'Proof of an External World', in 'Philosophical
Papers', (Allen & Unwin, 1959) pp. 127—50; reprinted
from the 'Proceedings of the British Academy', xxv (1939)
273—300.
Alice Ambrose, 'Moore's Proof of an External World', in Paul
Arthur Schilpp (ed.), 'The Philosophy of G. E. Moore', 2nd
ed. (New York: Tudor Publishing Company, 1952) pp.
395—418.

The enterprise of proving God's existence

Austin Farrer, 'Finite and Infinite', 2nd ed. (Dacre Press,
1959) Part I.
George I. Mavrodes, 'Belief in God', chap. ii.
James F. Ross, 'Philosophical Theology', chap. i.
J. J. C. Smart, 'The Existence of God', in Flew and MacIntyre,
'New Essays in Philosophical Theology', pp. 28—46.

Discussions of traditional theistic arguments

D. R. Burrill (ed.), 'The Cosmological Arguments' (New York:
Doubleday, 1967).
Karl Barth, 'Anselm: Fides Quaerens Intellectum', trans.
Robertson (S.C.M. Press, 1960).
John Hick and Arthur C. McGill (eds), 'The Many-Faced
Argument' (New York: Macmillan, 1967).
David Hume, 'Dialogues Concerning Natural Religion', many
editions.
Wallace, I. Matson, 'The Existence of God' (Ithaca, N.Y.:
Cornell U.P., 1965).
E. L. Mascall, 'Existence and Analogy', (London and New
York: Longmans, Green, 1949).
E. L. Mascall, 'Faith and Reason: Anselm and Aquinas', in

178

'Journal of Theological Studies', new series, xiv (1963) 67—90.

E. L. Mascall, 'He Who Is: A Study in Traditional Theism' (London and New York: Longmans, Green, 1943) (B).

Terence Penelhum, 'Religion and Rationality', Part I.

Alvin Plantinga, 'God and Other Minds', Part I.

Alvin Plantinga (ed.), 'The Ontological Argument' (Garden City, N.Y.: Doubleday, 1967).

On attempted disproofs of God's existence

J. N. Findlay, 'Can God's Existence be Disproved?', with rejoinders by G. E. Hughes and A. C. A. Rainer, in Flew and MacIntyre, 'New Essays in Philosophical Theology', pp. 47—75; reprinted from 'Mind' (1948).

John Hick, 'Evil and the God of Love' (London: Macmillan; New York: St Martin's Press, 1966).

E. H. Madden and Peter H. Hare, 'Evil and the Concept of God' (Springfield, Ill.: Charles C. Thomas, 1968).

Terence Penelhum, 'Divine Goodness and the Problem of Evil', in 'Religious Studies', ii (1966) 95—107.

Nelson Pike (ed.), 'God and Evil' (Englewood Cliffs, N.J.: Prentice-Hall, 1964).

The possibility of metaphysics

D. F. Pears (ed.), 'The Nature of Metaphysics' (London: Macmillan; New York: St Martin's Press, 1957).

Ian Ramsey (ed.), 'Prospect for Metaphysics'(London: Allen & Unwin; New York: Philosophical Library, 1961).

W. H. Walsh, 'Metaphysics' (Hutchinson, 1963).

The distinction between theistic and non-theistic statements

Gareth B. Matthews, 'Theology and Natural Theology', in 'Journal of Philosophy', lxi (1964) 99—108.

Bertrand Russell, 'On Denoting', in Feigl and Sellars (eds), 'Readings in Philosophical Analysis' (New York: Appleton-Century-Crofts, 1949) pp. 103—15; reprinted from 'Mind' (1905).

P. F. Strawson, 'On Referring', in G. H. R. Parkinson (ed.),
'The Theory of Meaning' (Oxford University Press, 1968)
pp. 61—85 (B).

Chapter 4

Verificationism

W. P. Alston, 'Philosophy of Language' (Englewood Cliffs,
N.J.: Prentice-Hall, 1964) chap. 4.
A. J. Ayer, 'Language, Truth and Logic' (Gollancz, (1936).
Carl G. Hempel, 'Problems and Changes in the Empiricist
Criterion of Meaning', in C.G. Hempel, 'Aspects of
Scientific Explanation' (New York: Free Press, 1966);
reprinted from 'Revue Internationale de Philosophie'
(1950).
Norman Malcolm, 'The Verification Argument', in Max Black
(ed.), 'Philosophical Analysis' Ithaca, N.Y.: Cornell U.P.,
1950) pp. 244—98.
F. Waismann, 'Verifiability', in his 'How I See Philosophy',
ed. R. Harré (London: Macmillan; New York: St Martin's
Press, 1968) pp. 39—66.

Theological positivism

Antony Flew, et al., 'Theology and Falsification', in 'New
Essays in Philosophical Theology'.
John Wilson, 'Philosophy and Religion' (Oxford University
Press, 1961).

Theological phenomenalism

R. B. Braithwaite, 'An Empiricist's View of the Nature of
Religious Belief', in I.T. Ramsey (ed), 'Christian Ethics and
Contemporary Philosophy' (S.C.M. Press, 1966) pp.
53—73; reprinted from pamphlet published by the Cambridge University Press (1955).
David Cox, 'The Significance of Christianity', in 'Mind', lx
(1950) pp. 209—18.
E. L. Mascall, 'The Secularisation of Christianity' (Longmans,
1965).

T. R. Miles, 'Religion and the Scientific Outlook' (Allen & Unwin, 1959).

B. Murchland (ed.), 'The Meaning of the Death of God' (New York: Vintage Books, Random House, 1967).

J. A. T. Robinson, 'Honest to God' (S.C.M. Press, 1963).

Paul van Buren, 'The Secular Meaning of the Gospel' (S.C.M. Press, 1963).

Eschatological verifications

John Hick, 'Faith and Knowledge', chap. 8.

John Hick, 'Theology and Verification', in 'Theology Today' xvii (1960) 12–31.

George Mavrodes, 'God and Verification', in 'Canadian Journal of Theology', x (1964) 187–91.

Kai Nielsen, 'Eschatological Verification', in 'Canadian Journal of Theology', ix (1963) 271–81.

Kai Nielsen, 'God and Verification Again', in 'Canadian Journal of Theology', xi (1965) 135–41.

Terence Penelhum, 'Survival and Disembodied Existence' (London: Routledge & Kegan Paul; New York: Humanities Press, 1970) (B).

Chapter 5

The concept of revelation

John Baillie, 'Our Knowledge of God' (New York: Scribner's, 1959).

*John Baillie, 'The Idea of Revelation in Recent Thought', (New York: Columbia U.P., 1956) (B).

Karl Barth, 'Church Dogmatics', Vol. I, Part I, 'The Doctrine of the Word of God', trans. G. T. Thomson (New York: Scribner's, 1936).

Karl Barth, 'The Word of God and the Word of Man', trans. Horton (New York: Harper, 1957).

Emil Brunner, 'The Philosophy of Religion' (Clarke, 1958).

C. H. Dodd, 'The Authority of the Bible' (London: Nisbet, 1929; New York: Harper, 1929 and 1958).

Austin Farrer, 'Revelation', in Basil Mitchell (ed.), 'Faith and Logic', pp. 84–107.

181

Antony Flew, 'God and Philosophy', chaps. 6–8.
Ronald W. Hepburn, 'Christianity and Paradox', chaps. v–vi.
John Hick, 'Revelation', in Paul Edwards, 'Encyclopedia of Philosophy', vii 189–91 (B).
H. R. Niebuhr, 'The Meaning of Revelation' (New York: Macmillan, 1946).

Religious experience

W. P. Alston, 'Psychoanalytic Theory and Theistic Belief', in John Hick (ed.), 'Faith and the Philosophers', pp. 63–102.
Ronald W. Hepburn, 'Christianity and Paradox', chaps. ii, iv, xi.
Marghanita Laski, 'Ecstasy' (Cresset Press, 1961).
R. S. Lee, 'Freud and Christianity' (Clarke, 1948; Penguin Books, 1967).
H. D. Lewis, 'Our Experience of God' (London: Allen & Unwin; New York: Macmillan, 1959).
Rudolf Otto, 'The Idea of the Holy', 2nd ed., trans. Harvey (Oxford University Press, 1950).

Chapter 6

The nature of faith

D. M. Baillie, 'Faith in God' (Faber & Faber, 1964).
Martin Buber, 'Two Types of Faith', trans. Goldhawk (New York: Harper, 1961).
John Hick, 'Faith', in Paul Edwards, 'Encyclopedia of Philosophy', iii (B).
Søren Kierkegaard, 'Fear and Trembling', trans. Lowrie (Princetown U.P., 1941; Garden City, N.Y.: Anchor Books, Doubleday, 1954).
Søren Kierkegaard, 'Concluding Unscientific Postscript', trans. Lowrie (Princetown U.P., 1963).
Søren Kierkegaard, 'Philosophical Fragments', trans. Swenson (Princetown U.P., 1962).
Paul Tillich, 'Dynamics of Faith' (New York: Harper, 1957).

Knowledge and belief

Roderick M. Chisholm, 'Theory of Knowledge' (Englewood

Cliffs, N.J.: Prentice-Hall, 1966).

A. Phillips Griffiths (ed.), 'Knowledge and Belief' (Oxford University Press, 1967) (B).

Charles Landesman (ed.), 'The Foundation of Knowledge' (Englewood Cliffs, N.J.: Prentice-Hall, 1970) (B).

H. H. Price, 'Belief' (London: Allen & Unwin; New York: Humanities Press, 1969).

Appendices

Self-deception

John V. Canfield and Don F. Gustavson, 'Self-Deception', in 'Analysis', xxiii (1962) 32—6.

Herbert Fingarette, 'Self-Deception' (London: Routledge & Kegan Paul; New York: Humanities Press, 1969) (B).

Patrick Gardiner, 'Error, Faith, and Self-Deception', in 'Proceedings of the Aristotelian Society' (1969—70) pp. 221—43.

Terence Penelhum, 'Pleasure and Falsity', in 'American Philosophical Quarterly', i (1964) 1—11; reprinted in Stuart Hampshire (ed.),'Philosphy of Mind' (New York: Harper & Row, 1966) pp. 242—66.

Pascal's Wager

Antony Flew, 'Is Pascal's Wager the Only Safe Bet?', in 'Rationalist Annual' (London, 1960) pp. 21—5.

Ernest Mortimer, 'Blaise Pascal' (Methuen, 1959).

Denzil Patrick, 'Pascal and Kierkegaard' (Lutterworth Press, 1947) i.

Terence Penelhum, 'Pascal's Wager', in 'Journal of Religion', xliv (1964) 201—09.

Testimony and the miraculous

C. D. Broad, 'Hume's Theory of the Credibility of Miracles', in 'Proceedings of the Aristotelian Society', xvii (1916—17) 77—94; reprinted in Sesonske and Fleming (eds), 'Human Understanding' (Belmont, Calif.: Wadsworth, 1965) pp. 86—98.

Antony Flew, 'Hume's Philosophy of Belief' (London: Routledge & Kegan Paul; New York: Humanities Press, 1961)
chap. viii.

David Hume, 'Enquiry Concerning Human Understanding',
Section X. Many editions.

C. S. Lewis, 'Miracles' (Fontana Books, Collins, 1960).

Richard R. Niebuhr, 'Resurrection and Historical Reason'
(New York: Scribner's, 1957).

Michael C. Perry, 'The Easter Enigma' (Faber & Faber,
1949).

I. T. Ramsey, et al., 'The Miracles and the Resurrection'
(S.P.C.K., 1964).

D. J. West, 'Eleven Lourdes Miracles' (Duckworth, 1957).

Index